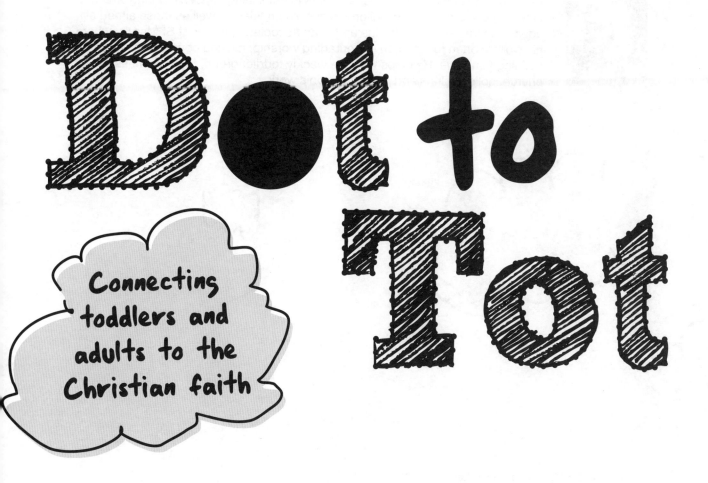

Dot to Tot

Connecting toddlers and adults to the Christian faith

Sue Merrifield and Rev Matt Taylor

CWR

Dot to Tot was written, and tried and tested, by Sue Merrifield and Rev Matt Taylor from St Mary's Church, Rushden.

Sue has a long history of working with young children. As well as raising her own four children, she worked as a childminder, playgroup leader and Early Years teacher. She was also a part-time advisor for Northamptonshire Education Authority. She has worshipped at St Mary's for many years and has been a Sunday club leader, run holiday clubs and Messy Church.

Rev Matt Taylor worked for over 20 years in publishing for CWR, during which time he helped to develop Children's and Youth titles as well as those aimed at adults. He trained at St Mellitus and is an Associate Minister at St Mary's, where his work is often focused on encouraging worship, making connections and building family life. He helps with the weekly toddler group, monthly messy-style church, holiday clubs and regular schools work.

Contents

Using Dot to Tot

What's it all about?

We all love to be connected. Every day, we connect with people face to face, over the phone or through social media, and even the most fleeting of connections can leave their mark on us.

Parent and toddler groups provide a space for toddlers to start making those connections themselves (and for the parents to talk with someone whose main concern is not CBeebies!).

For churches, these groups can be a great way of providing a bridge for people who would not consider themselves 'church-goers'. Both parents and toddlers can form friendships, connecting Christians with those in their community and vice versa.

Dot to Tot started with one parent and toddler group (led by Sue Merrifield and Rev Matt Taylor) who saw the opportunity to take this further and connect both toddler and parent directly to biblical truths. From their experience and tried-and-tested material, this resource was created. It is made up of three terms' worth of adaptable sessions, incorporating two key features: one to help connect toddlers with God and the other to help parents. Here's how you can facilitate this in your own group …

Connecting toddlers ...

Each week includes a Bible-based story time and activity that are designed to be used during your group meeting. You will see these are split into four sections: **Attention grabber**, **Puppet intro**, **Story time** and **Things to make and do**.

The **Attention grabber** is the same each week and is simply suggested to be used for grabbing the children's attention. It may be a good idea to gather all the children together, in the same place, at the beginning of each group and sing this together. Alternatively, you could always create your own version!

Next up is the **Puppet intro**. Children love a puppet! And they love them even more when they 'get to know them' so why not use the same puppet every week and introduce it with a name of your choice? You could use a puppet, teddy bear or toy.

The **Story time** story is either based on a particular Bible story or wider biblical theme. These come with actions (highlighted in bold) to help engage the children and get them involved. It might be a good idea to read the story and practise the actions in preparation before the group, to familiarise yourself with them.

If you like to include an activity during your group then the **Things to make and do** suggestions are there to help consolidate what the children have learnt during story time. Read though these before your group starts to see if you need to prepare anything.

Connecting parents ...

So that parents (or carers) might think about that day's story and how it could apply to them personally, accompanying each weekly plan is a photocopiable handout for you to copy and give out to them.

These handouts are designed to help adults raise their heads up from the tasks of parenting for a moment and make a personal connection with God. They include the **Story time** stories for their reference, a quick explanation and thought-provoking idea surrounding that story, and a Bible verse.

You may choose to hand these out at the end of the group or perhaps during the more social time of coffee and playtime, when you could also take the opportunity to connect and chat to a parent.

Week 1

You are loved

Attention grabber

Wiggle your fingers
Pat your knees
Fold your arms
And look at me!

Puppet intro

Here is [puppet's name].

Children, can you say 'Hello, [puppet's name]'?

Wait for children to respond.

I love [puppet's name] and [he/she] loves me.

Who do you love? Do you love your mummy? Do you love your daddy? Do you love your sister? Do you love your brother? How do you show them that you love them?

Pause for children to think.

Today we are going to hear from the Bible, about how Jesus loves us all the time.

Story time

Jesus loves me when I play. **Jump up and down.**

Jesus loves me when I walk. **Walk forwards and back.**

Jesus loves me when I run about. **Run on the spot.**

Jesus loves me when I sleep. **Lie down or place your hands together and under your head.**

Jesus loves me when I'm sad. **Pull a sad face.**

Jesus loves me when I'm happy. **Pull a happy face.**

The Bible tells me that Jesus loves me all the time. **Open arms wide.**

That's the end of the story. Shall we do it again so you can all join in with the actions?

Repeat the story.

Things to make and do

You will need:
A heart-shaped template
A4 card (white or colour)
Scissors
Crayons
Paint, pens, glitter, stickers (optional)

Before the group starts use the template, scissors and card to cut out card hearts.

During the group give out card hearts and crayons (and additional materials if desired), and encourage the children to decorate their card heart. When they have finished, suggest that they take the heart home so that it will remind them of how Jesus loves them all the time.

You are loved

Your child heard this story today ...

Jesus loves me when I play. Jesus loves me when I walk. Jesus loves me when I run about. Jesus loves me when I sleep. Jesus loves me when I'm sad. Jesus loves me when I'm happy. The Bible tells me that Jesus loves me all the time.

Here's a thought ...

There are over 1,200 pop songs with love in the title. We love to be loved. Children thrive when they know they are safe and loved. Adults really aren't any different. The Bible says we all are children of God. His love for us, as the story today says, is never-ending and extravagant.

'See what great love the Father has lavished on us, that we should be called children of God! And that is what we are!' (1 John 3:1)

Week 2

Who is Jesus?

Attention grabber

Wiggle your fingers
Pat your knees
Fold your arms
And look at me!

Puppet intro

Who is this? **Point at the puppet.**

Who is this? **Point at yourself.**

How do you know? Because someone told you? Or because you got to know them?

Pause for children to think.

Our story today is about when Jesus' friends, the disciples, found out who Jesus really is.

Story time

Jesus was with His friends, the disciples.
Mimic talking hands.

He said, 'Who do people say I am?'

They told Him, 'Some say John the Baptist.'

Shake your head with each 'no'.

NO! NO! NO!

'Some say Elijah.'

NO! NO! NO!

'Some say a prophet.'

NO! NO! NO!

Jesus said, 'Who do you think I am?'

Peter said, 'You are Jesus Christ, the Son of God.'

Nod your head with each 'yes'.

YES! YES! YES! Peter knew who Jesus was and so do we. HOORAY!

That's the end of the story. Shall we do it again so you can all join in with the actions?

Repeat the story.

This story is found in Mark 8:27–29

Things to make and do

You will need:
Large coloured card (to make crowns)
A stapler
Scissors
Crayons
Glitter, stickers, pom poms (optional)

Before the group starts cut long, thick strips of the card out to make the flat crowns, and cut a zig-zag down one length of each one.

During the group give out the flat crowns, crayons (and additional materials if desired), and encourage the children to decorate the crowns. When they have finished, bend the crown around their heads to fit and then take the crown off and staple the edges together. Suggest that they take the crowns home to remind them that Jesus is King!

Who is Jesus?

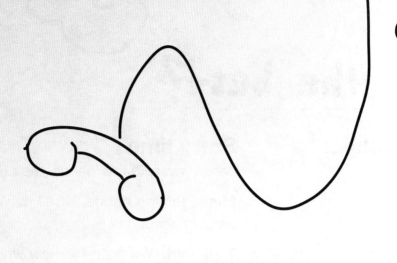

Your child heard this story today …

Jesus was with His friends, the disciples. He said, 'Who do people say I am?'

They told Him, 'Some say John the Baptist.'

'Some say Elijah.'

'Some say a prophet.'

Jesus said, 'Who do you think I am?'

Peter said, 'You are Jesus Christ, the Son of God.' Peter knew who Jesus was and so do we.

This story is found in Mark 8:27–29

Here's a thought …

When we get a knock on the door or the phone rings, the question immediately comes into our heads: 'Who is it?'

Often we can tell by someone's voice who that person is. We smile and say, 'Hi'. We know them. Peter had lived alongside Jesus, he knew who He was.

How about you? Who do you think Jesus is?

"But what about you?" he asked. "Who do you say I am?" Peter answered, "You are the Messiah." (Mark 8:29)

Week 3

Who's the best?

Attention grabber

Wiggle your fingers
Pat your knees
Fold your arms
And look at me!

Puppet intro

What's that, [puppet's name]?
Puppet whispers in your ear.

You want to know who's the best out of you and me?

Hmmm? What a funny question!

Our story today is about when Jesus' friends, the disciples, were arguing about who is the best.

Story time

Jesus was with His friends, the disciples.

Mimic talking hands. He said, 'What are you arguing about?'

They said, 'We want to know which one of us is the best.'

Put right hand up. 'ME?'

Shake head and bring hand down. No.

Put left hand up. 'ME?'

Shake head and bring hand down. No.

Put right hand up. 'ME?'

Shake head and bring hand down. No.

'Who then?'

Jesus picked up a little child, just like you, and said, 'You have to be like this if you want to please God. Not bossy or showing off. Just like a little child.'

That's the end of the story. Shall we do it again so you can all join in with the actions?

Repeat the story.

This story is found in Mark 9:33–37

Things to make and do

Play this variation of the traditional children's game 'Duck, Duck, Goose'.

During the group ask the children to sit in a circle and choose one to walk around the outside, tapping each child's head and saying 'Disciple'. When they tap someone on the head and say 'Child', that child will chase them around the outside of the circle. If they sit down in that child's place before they are caught, then they stay there and the other child starts the 'Disciple, Disciple, Child' game again. Play until every child that wants a turn has had one. At the end of the game remind the children that Jesus told the disciples not to show off or be bossy, but to be like a child, and that would make God happy.

Who's the best?

Your child heard this story today ...

Jesus was with His friends, the disciples. He said, 'What are you arguing about?'

They said, 'We want to know which one of us is the best.'

'ME?' No.

'ME?' No.

'ME?' No.

'Who then?'

Jesus picked up a little child, and said, 'You have to be like this if you want to please God. Not bossy or showing off. Just like a little child.'

This story is found in Mark 9:33–37

Here's a thought ...

Sometimes when some blokes get together there can be a bit of competition. Their inner Ray Winstone comes out – 'Who's the daddy?' But actually we can all be a bit like that sometimes. *We know best, we know better, we know* that lies somewhere deep inside us.

Jesus tells us that when it comes to faith, sometimes we need to be like a little child. We have to admit that, next to God – the Creator of the universe – we don't really know better.

'Trust in the LORD with all your heart and lean not on your own understanding; in all your ways submit to him, and he will make your paths straight.' (Proverbs 3:5–6)

Week 4 Harvest Festival

Wonderful world

Attention grabber

Wiggle your fingers
Pat your knees
Fold your arms
And look at me!

Puppet intro

Hello, [puppet's name]. Did you
know that God made the world?

Puppet nods.

That's right. He made the flowers
and trees and the food that grows.

This Sunday, we celebrate
Harvest Festival, and we will all
say 'Thank You' to God for all
that He gives us.

*Today we are going to say thanks
in our story time.*

Story time

Thank You, God, for night and day.

Mimic sleeping and then being awake.

Thank You, God, for flowers and trees.

Stand up like a tree.

Thank You, God, for food and drink.

Rub your tummy.

Thank You, God, for families to love.

Give someone a hug.

Thank You, God, for loving us.

Wrap your arms around yourself.

Thank You, God, for harvest time.

Clap and say, 'Hooray!'

That's the end of the story. Shall we do it again so
you can all join in the actions?

Repeat the story.

The story of creation is found in Genesis 1–2

Things to make and do

You will need:
Harvest themed colouring-in sheets
Crayons

Before the group starts search the internet
for colouring-in sheets based on harvest
time, then download and print out copies of
your preferred one/s.

During the group give out the sheets and
crayons for the children to colour in. At the
end, encourage the children to take their
sheet/s home with them as a reminder that
God made everything for us – and how
thankful we are!

Wonderful world

Your child heard this story today ...

Thank You, God, for night and day.
Thank You, God, for flowers and
trees. Thank You, God, for food and
drink. Thank You, God, for families to
love. Thank You, God, for loving us.
Thank You, God, for harvest time.

The story of creation is found in Genesis 1–2

Here's a thought ...

An acceptance speech at the Oscars
can seem to go on for hours. Gwyneth
Paltrow's famous tearful speech in 1999
set the gold standard for mentioning the
most people in the Western world who
knew her. But saying thank you is a good
thing. We were taught that as a child; we
teach that to our children. So what about
the One who holds the universe together,
gives us breath and enables the crops to
grow? Isn't God the One really deserving
of all our thanks?

'You care for the land and water it; you
enrich it abundantly. The streams of God
are filled with water to provide the people
with corn' (Psalm 65:9)

Week 5

Seen and heard

Attention grabber

Wiggle your fingers
Pat your knees
Fold your arms
And look at me!

Puppet intro

[Puppet's name], look I have a baby. This is [baby doll's name]. I love babies.

Mummies and daddies really love their babies, too.

Now, what are you? Are you a child?

Do you know any other children?

Are there any other children in your family?

Well, Jesus loves all of you.

How do we know? It says so in a very special book called the Bible.

Today our story is about how much Jesus loves children like you.

Story time

Jesus was with His friends, the disciples.

Some people brought their children to meet Jesus. **Beckon with a gesture.**

Jesus' friends told them to go away. **Shake head and wave away.**

But Jesus said, 'Let the little children come to me.' **Beckon with a gesture.**

And He held them and loved them. **Rock arms.**

Jesus loves children.

That's the end of the story. Shall we do it again so you can all join in with the actions?

Repeat the story.

This story is found in Mark 10:13–16

Things to make and do

You will need:

Gingerbread child colouring-in sheets
Crayons
Glitter, stickers, pom poms, string, glue (optional)

Before the group starts search the internet for images of a simple line drawing of a gingerbread child and download and print out copies.

During the group give out the sheets and crayons (and additional materials if desired), and encourage the children to decorate the picture so that it looks like them. Tell them to think about what colour hair and eyes they have, and what clothes they're wearing. When they have finished, suggest that they take their picture home so that it will remind them that they are very special to Jesus.

Seen and heard

AAAHH!

Your child heard this story today …

Jesus was with His friends, the disciples. Some people brought their children to meet Jesus. Jesus' friends told them to go away. But Jesus said, 'Let the little children come to me.' And He held them and loved them. Jesus loves children.

This story is found in Mark 10:13–16

Here's a thought …

Have you ever been in a shop with your child when they have thrown a tantrum? Face down, legs kicking – the looks people give! Children, after all, should be 'seen and not heard'! Well, this was not Jesus' way.

Though children in His day were not valued highly by society, Jesus loved them and wanted them to spend time with Him. And their simple receptive openness He wanted to encourage in us too. Can we, sometimes, be too 'grown-up' to listen to Him?

'Jesus said, "Let the little children come to me, and do not hinder them, for the kingdom of heaven belongs to such as these."' (Matthew 19:14)

Week 6

Count on it

Attention grabber

Wiggle your fingers
Pat your knees
Fold your arms
And look at me!

Puppet intro

Are you good at counting,
[puppet's name]?

Puppet voice: 1, 3, 2, 4.

Oh, [he/she] isn't very good!

Let's help [him/her]. 1, 2, 3, 4.
Good!

Today's story is about counting.

Story time

In the Bible, Jesus tells us that God is very good
at counting.

Count all the children (or a small group of them).

He knows all of us by name.

Name two or three of the children.

He knows if we are happy **smile** or sad **frown**.

He loves us all. **Put hands on heart.**

He even counts the hairs on our heads!

Pat head.

That's the end of the story. Shall we do it again so you
can all join in with the actions?

Repeat the story.

Things to make and do

You will need:
Face colouring-in sheets
Wool (in different 'hair' colours)
Scissors
Glue
Crayons

Before the group starts search the internet
for images of a simple line drawing of a
smiling face. Download your preferred one
and print out copies. Also cut out short
lengths of wool, which will be stuck on the
sheets to make the hair.

During the group give out the colouring-in
sheets, crayons, glue and short lengths of
wool. Encourage the children to colour in
the face and stick on the 'hair'. When they
have finished, ask the children to count how
many hairs they have put on their picture.
Suggest that they take their picture home
to remind them that God knows how many
hairs they have on their head – which shows
that He loves us very much.

Count on it

Your child heard this story today ...

In the Bible, Jesus tells us that God is very good at counting. He knows all of us by name. He knows if we are happy or sad. He loves us all. He even counts the hairs on our heads!

Here's a thought ...

Depending on the quality of our eyesight, the notion of God being able to count the hairs on our heads is slightly less impressive for some of us than for others! But the truth that God cares and knows us so intimately is amazing. Maybe we have the idea that God is at a distance, only faintly interested in us, distracted by running the universe. But the Bible tells us otherwise. Not only does God know our names, He knows and cares about the minute details of our lives. That's quite an incredible concept to really grasp.

'even the very hairs of your head are all numbered.' (Matthew 10:30)

Week 7
Lost and found

Attention grabber

Wiggle your fingers
Pat your knees
Fold your arms
And look at me!

Puppet intro

Do you know your animals?
[Puppet's name] loves making
animal noises.

Puppet voice: Mooo!

What's this?

Wait for children to respond.

That's right, a cow!

Puppet voice: Baaaa!

What about that one?

Wait for children to respond.

Yes, it's a sheep!

*Today's story is one that Jesus
told about a sheep that got lost.*

Story time

There was once a shepherd who had lots of sheep.

Show and wiggle all your fingers.

One day, one of the sheep got lost.

Hold up index finger.

The shepherd looked everywhere.

Stand up and look around but not at your finger.

At last the sheep was found.

Look at your finger.

The shepherd was very happy.

Clap and say, 'Hooray!'

Jesus told lots of good stories.

That's the end of the story. Shall we do it again so you
can all join in with the actions?

Repeat the story.

This story is found in Luke 15:3–7

Things to make and do

You will need:
Sheep colouring-in sheets
Cotton wool
Glue
Crayons

Before the group starts search the internet
for images of a simple line drawing of a
sheep. Download your preferred one and
print out copies.

During the group give out the sheets,
crayons, cotton wool and glue. Encourage
the children to colour in their picture and
then stick the cotton wool to the sheep's
body. When they have finished, suggest
that they take their sheep home to remind
them that we are like sheep and Jesus is our
caring Shepherd.

Lost and found

Your child heard this story today …

There was once a shepherd who had lots of sheep. One day, one of the sheep got lost. The shepherd looked everywhere. At last the sheep was found. The shepherd was very happy. Jesus told lots of good stories.

This story is found in Luke 15:3–7

Here's a thought …

When we lose something, often someone will ask us, 'Where did you last leave it?' Surely if we knew that, we'd know where it is, right?! Searching for something we've lost can be frustrating, stressful and even upsetting.

One of the unique truths about the Christian faith is that it's not about finding God. We think of all religions as humankind's search for God, but the Bible tells us that, actually, God searches for us. God sent His Son to find us, His lost sheep, and He keeps on until we are found. That is unless we are determined to hide.

'For God so loved the world that he gave his one and only Son, that whoever believes in him shall not perish but have eternal life.' (John 3:16)

Week 8
Halloween and Bonfire Night

Not afraid

Attention grabber

Wiggle your fingers
Pat your knees
Fold your arms
And look at me!

Puppet intro

Puppet shivering.

What's wrong, [puppet's name]?

Puppet whispers in your ear.

You're scared? What of?

Puppet whispers in your ear.

Pumpkins and fireworks! Well, yes, I suppose it is the time of year for Halloween and Bonfire Night, isn't it?

Our story today tells us that we don't need to ever be scared.

Story time

Jesus was with His friends and they were worried because they thought He was going away for good.

Pull a sad face and say, 'Oh dear!'

But Jesus said, 'You never need to be worried or afraid. I am going to be with you always!'

That is good news, isn't it? We don't need to worry about Halloween.

Throw your hands up and say, 'Boo!'

We don't need to be scared of fireworks.

Jump up and say, 'Bang!'

Or anything! Because we have Jesus with us forever and ever.

Clap and say, 'Hooray!'

That's the end of the story. Shall we do it again so you can all join in with the actions?

Repeat the story.

This story is found in Matthew 28:16–20

Things to make and do

You will need:
Pumpkin/Fireworks colouring-in sheets
Crayons

Before the group starts search the internet for colouring-in sheets of a pumpkin with a happy face and another of fireworks. Download your preferred ones and print out copies.

During the group give out the sheets and crayons for the children to colour in. At the end, encourage the children to take their sheet/s home to remind them that we do not need to be afraid because God is with us.

Not afraid

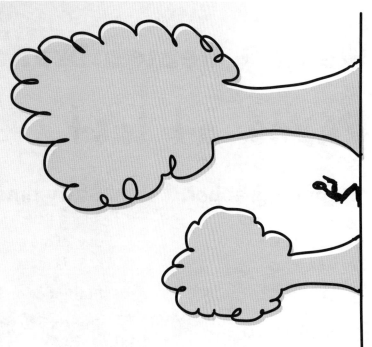

Your child heard this story today …

Jesus was with His friends and they were worried because they thought He was going away for good. But Jesus said, 'You never need to be worried or afraid. I am going to be with you always!' That is good news, isn't it? We don't need to worry about Halloween. We don't need to be scared of fireworks. Or anything! Because we have Jesus with us forever and ever!

This story is found in Matthew 28:16–20

Here's a thought …

We might not be scared of the same things our children are scared of, but how often do we worry about our children? No matter how old we are, how safe or stable we feel, we all get scared or worried about things from time to time.

Jesus understands first-hand how we feel. He certainly knew what fear was when He knelt in the Garden of Gethsemane and waited to face a most painful death.

Jesus is with us. He loves us passionate y and longs for us to hand our fears over to Him. What fears or worries can you give to Jesus today?

'Cast all your anxiety on him because he cares for you.' (1 Peter 5:7)

Week 9 Remembrance Sunday
Peace at last

Attention grabber

Wiggle your fingers
Pat your knees
Fold your arms
And look at me!

Puppet intro

Pin a poppy onto the puppet.

What is [puppet's name] wearing?

Wait for children to respond.

That's right! It's a poppy!

We wear poppies for Remembrance Sunday, which is when we remember all the people and soldiers who died in the wars.

Today's story is about the poppies, peace and Jesus.

Story time

A long time ago, on the eleventh hour, of the eleventh day, of the eleventh month, the guns stopped firing and all was quiet.

Put finger on lips and say, 'Shh!'

The war was over and all the soldiers could go home.

Clap and say, 'Hooray!'

Jesus is the Prince of Peace.

Mimic putting a crown on your head.

Peace means no war or fighting. Jesus said we should love each other, not fight.

Hug someone.

Poppies remind us of peace. Peace reminds us of Jesus.

That's the end of the story. Shall we do it again so you can all join in with the actions?

Repeat the story.

Things to make and do

You will need:
Red tissue paper
Green pipe cleaners
Black beads

Before the group starts cut circles out of the red tissue paper and glue a black bead to the end of each pipe cleaner. You will be making poppies with the children so make one as an example of how it will look. Place a few circles of tissue paper together and where they join in the centre, pierce a pipe cleaner through all the way to the bead, then bend the pipe cleaner down to look like a stalk. If needed, secure petals to the pipe cleaner with glue or sticky tape.

During the group give out the tissue paper and pipe cleaners with beads, and show the children each step of making the poppy. The children may need help as they go, so perhaps ask some helpers or parents to help. When they have finished, suggest that they take it home so that it will remind them of peace and of Jesus.

Peace at last

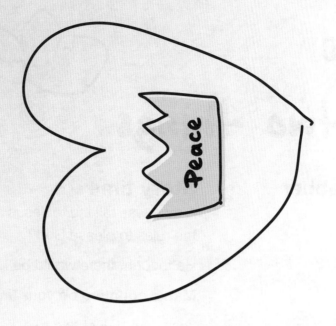

Your child heard this story today ...

A long time ago, on the eleventh hour, of the eleventh day, of the eleventh month, the guns stopped firing and all was quiet. The war was over and all the soldiers could go home.

Jesus is the Prince of Peace. Peace means no war or fighting. Jesus said we should love each other, not fight. Poppies remind us of peace. Peace reminds us of Jesus.

Here's a thought ...

John Lennon tried to imagine a world at peace (and wrote a great song at the same time!). Isaiah, a man in the Bible, beat him to it some 2,800 years earlier. The big difference was that Lennon tried to imagine a universe without God. Isaiah saw God as the One who would one day bring about final lasting peace.

That is why one of the titles given to Jesus is 'Prince of Peace'. As God's Son, He started that peace process in our hearts that will one day be completed for the whole world when He returns again. Can you imagine that?

'They will beat their swords into ploughshares and their spears into pruning hooks. Natior will not take up sword against nation, nor will they train for war any more.' (Isaiah 2:4)

© Dot to Tot

Week 10

Just two things

Attention grabber

Wiggle your fingers
Pat your knees
Fold your arms
And look at me!

Puppet intro

Me and [puppet's name] crossed the road today. Did you cross a road today?

Wait for children to respond.

There are rules to keep us safe when crossing the road.

Puppet nods.

That's right. There are three things to remember:

Stop. **Hold out palm of hand.**

Look. **You and puppet look left to right.**

And listen. **Put hand to ear.**

Today's story is about two very important rules that Jesus taught people in the Bible.

Story time

A man was talking to Jesus and he said, 'What are the rules to please God?'

He thought there would be lots.

Mimic counting on your fingers.

Jesus said, 'Just two rules!'

Hold up two fingers.

'What are they?' asked the man.

Jesus said, 'Number one.' **One finger.**

'Love God.' **Hand on heart then point up.**

'Number two.' **Two fingers.**

'Love each other.' **Hand on heart then point to children.**

That's the end of the story. Shall we do it again so you can all join in with the actions?

Repeat the story.

This story is found in Matthew 22:34–40

Things to make and do

Play a game called 'Stop, Look, Listen'.

During the group tell the children to walk around the room. When you say 'Stop', they need to freeze where they are. When you say 'Look', they need to look at you. And when you say 'Listen', they need to touch their ears. If you like, you could call children out who were the last to respond until you have one 'winner'. You could also do a round where they have to walk faster or run. Remind them at the end that rules are very important and that Jesus gave us two rules: to love God and to love each other.

Just two things

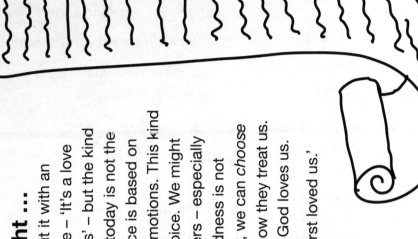

Your child heard this story today ...

A man was talking to Jesus and he said, 'What are the rules to please God?' He thought there would be lots. Jesus said, 'Just two rules!'

'What are they?' asked the man.

Jesus said, 'Number one, love God. Number two, love each other.'

This story is found in Matthew 22:34–40

Here's a thought ...

Taylor Swift sang about it with an infectiously catchy tune – 'It's a love story, baby just say yes' – but the kind of love we read about today is not the romantic kind! Romance is based on feelings, desires and emotions. This kind of love is based on choice. We might not *feel* like loving others – especially when our love and kindness is not reciprocated. However, we can *choose* to love them, despite how they treat us. Why? Simply because God loves us.

'We love because he first loved us.'
(1 John 4:19)

Week 11

Saw it coming

Attention grabber

Wiggle your fingers
Pat your knees
Fold your arms
And look at me!

Puppet intro

[Puppet's name] and I went for a walk the other day. We were looking out for birds with our binoculars. Binoculars help us to see things that are far, far away. Now, long, long before Jesus was born, there were people looking out for Him. We call these people prophets.

Our story today is about Isaiah, a prophet who was looking out for Jesus.

Story time

Long, long ago, there lived a man whose name was Isaiah. He was God's friend.

Shake hands with someone.

God talked to him and told him that one day He would send Jesus for us all.

Clap and say, 'Hooray!'

Isaiah said to all the people, 'Get ready, Jesus is coming. Keep looking out for Him!'

Mimic using binoculars.

That's the end of the story. Shall we do it again so you can all join in with the actions?

Repeat the story.

This story is found in Isaiah 7:13–14

Things to make and do

You will need:

Toilet roll cardboard tubes
Masking tape
Thick string/wool
Crayons
Tissue paper
Glue

Before the group starts make an example of what the children will be making, which will be a set of binoculars. Place two tubes together and wrap the tape around them so that they are securely taped together. Cut a length of string and stick each end to either side of the binoculars (this is so you can hang the binoculars around your neck). Colour in the binoculars or cover in tissue paper to decorate.

During the group give out the tubes, crayons, glue and tissue paper, and encourage the children to colour them in or cover them in tissue paper. As each child finishes, help them tape the tubes together and attach the string. When they have finished, get all the children to 'try out' their binoculars and say that we can be 'on the lookout' for Jesus.

Saw it coming

Your child heard this story today ...

Long, long ago, there lived a man whose name was Isaiah. He was God's friend. God talked to him and told him that one day He would send Jesus for us all. Isaiah said to all the people, 'Get ready, Jesus is coming. Keep looking out for Him!'

This story is found in Isaiah 7:13–14

Here's a thought ...

Isn't it great when children play hide and seek and instead of hiding they simply cover their eyes? They think that because they can't see you, you can't see them! Are there times in our lives when we wish we could actually do that?

Sometimes God wants us to know what's coming, as we see in today's story where the prophet, Isaiah, saw *who* was coming over 700 years before He was born! But then sometimes God just wants us to trust Him and His promise that He has good plans for our lives.

"For I know the plans I have for you," declares the LORD, "plans to prosper you and not to harm you, plans to give you hope and a future.'" (Jeremiah 29:11)

Week 12

Baby names

Attention grabber

Wiggle your fingers
Pat your knees
Fold your arms
And look at me!

Puppet intro

Puppet whispers in your ear.

[Puppet's name] is good at whispering. Can you whisper?

Why don't you whisper 'Hello' to [puppet's name]?

Wait for children to respond.

Sometimes people whisper when they have something special to say.

Today our story is about an angel who had something special to tell Mary.

Story time

Mary loved God. **Wrap your arms around yourself.**

God sent an angel to see Mary. **Spread arms wide.**

The angel had something very special to tell Mary. **Cup hand to mouth.**

The angel told Mary she was going to have a baby! **Mimic rocking a baby.**

The angel told Mary that the baby would be God's Son and His name would be Jesus. **Pull a surprised face and say, 'Wow!'**

That's the end of the story. Shall we do it again so you can all join in with the actions?

Repeat the story.

This story is found in Luke 1:26–38

Things to make and do

You will need:
Mary and angel colouring-in sheets
Crayons

Before the group starts search the internet for colouring-in sheets of Mary being visited by the angel. Download your preferred one and print out copies.

During the group give out the sheets and crayons for the children to colour in. At the end, encourage the children to take their sheet home to remind them of this special part in the Christmas story.

Baby names

Your child heard this story today ...

Mary loved God. God sent an angel to see Mary. The angel had something very special to tell Mary. The angel told Mary she was going to have a baby! The angel told Mary that the baby would be God's Son and His name would be Jesus.

This story is found in Luke 1:26–38

Here's a thought ...

Mary had been given some *incredible* news and an *incredible* name for her child (which is handy considering how long some of us spend choosing the names for our children!).

In Bible times, the meanings of names really, really meant something. Jesus (Joshua in Greek) means 'Saviour'. So it's no coincidence that millions of people have come to know Him as *their* Saviour.

This is a strange concept for some of us who don't particularly feel like we need saving. Saving from what? Aren't we fine as we are? What do you think?

'But when the kindness and love of God our Saviour appeared, he saved us, not because of righteous things we had done, but because of his mercy. He saved us ... so that, having been justified by his grace, we might become heirs having the hope of eternal life.' (Titus 3:4–7)

© Dot to Tot

Week 13

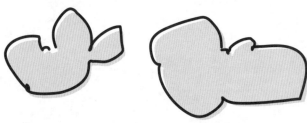

How wonder-full

Attention grabber
Wiggle your fingers
Pat your knees
Fold your arms
And look at me!

Puppet intro
[Puppet's name], this is [baby doll's name]. Isn't [he/she] cute? What do you think, children?

Wait for children to respond.

We were all babies once. Yes, even your mummy and daddy were babies! Mary and Joseph in the Bible had a very special baby.

Today our story is about when baby Jesus was born.

Story time
Mary and Joseph were tired. **Do a big yawn.**

The only place to sleep was a stable. **Pull a sad face.**

That night, baby Jesus was born! **Pull a happy face.**

Mary wrapped her baby up to keep Him warm. **Wrap your arms around yourself.**

He slept in a manger, which is a box filled with hay. **Put your hands under your head and pretend to sleep.**

Jesus is the King. **Mimic putting a crown on your head.**

But He came to earth as a little baby! **Mimic rocking a baby.**

That's the end of the story. Shall we do it again so you can all join in with the actions?

Repeat the story.

This story is found in Luke 2:4–7

Things to make and do
Play this variation of 'Duck, Duck, Goose'.

During the group ask the children to sit in a circle and choose one to walk around the outside, tapping each child's head and saying 'Baby'. When they tap someone on the head and say 'King', that child will chase them around the outside of the circle. If they sit down in that child's place before they are caught then they stay there and the other child starts the 'Baby, Baby, King' game again. Play until every child who wants a turn has had one. At the end of the game remind the children that Jesus is King, but He came to earth as a little baby.

How wonder-full

Your child heard this story today ...

Mary and Joseph were tired. The only place to sleep was a stable. That night, baby Jesus was born! Mary wrapped her baby up to keep Him warm. He slept in a manger, which is a box filled with hay. Jesus is the King. But He came to earth as a little baby!

This story is found in Luke 2:4–7

Here's a thought ...

Those who have experienced either giving birth or watching the birth of their son or daughter will know that great sense of wonder you feel when you first lay eyes on your baby.

God had a plan to bridge the gap between Himself and humankind so that we could have a relationship with Him, and it all began with a young girl giving birth to a baby. What wonder Mary must have felt when she looked down to see Jesus. What wonder could we experience too, if we let Jesus into our lives?

'Here I am! I stand at the door and knock. If anyone hears my voice and opens the door, I will come in' (Revelation 3:20)

Week 14

And now the good news

Attention grabber

Wiggle your fingers
Pat your knees
Fold your arms
And look at me!

Puppet intro

What's that, [puppet's name]?

Puppet whispers in your ear.

You have some news?

Puppet nods.

Well, what is it?

Puppet whispers in your ear.

You've got a new baby sister?

Puppet nods, very excitedly.

What brilliant news, thank you for telling me!

Today our story is about some very, very good news.

Story time

It was night time and some shepherds were taking care of their sheep. **Baaaa!**

The shepherds saw an angel! **Look up and point.**

The angel told them baby Jesus had been born. **Cup hands to mouth and shout, 'Good news!'**

The shepherds hurried off to go and find Him. **Run on the spot.**

The shepherds found Jesus in the stable with Mary and Joseph. **Kneel down.**

They were very pleased to see Him. **Big smile.**

So pleased in fact, they had to go and tell others the good news! **Run on the spot.**

That's the end of the story. Shall we do it again so you can all join in with the actions?

Repeat the story.

This story is found in Luke 2:8–20

Things to make and do

You will need:

Nativity scene colouring-in sheet
Crayons
Glitter, fabric scraps, cotton wool, glue (optional)

Before the group starts search the internet for colouring-in sheets of the nativity scene. Download your preferred one and print out copies.

During the group hand out the sheets and crayons (and additional materials if desired). Encourage the children to colour and decorate their nativity scene. When they have finished, suggest that they take it home so that they will be reminded of the good news of Jesus this Christmas!

And now the good news

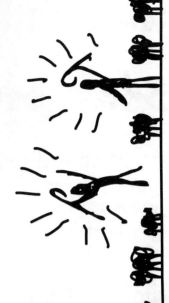

Your child heard this story today …

It was night time and some shepherds were taking care of their sheep. The shepherds saw an angel! The angel told them baby Jesus had been born. The shepherds hurried off to go and find Him. The shepherds found Jesus in the stable with Mary and Joseph. They were very pleased to see Him. So pleased in fact, they had to go and tell others the good news!

This story is found in Luke 2:8–20

Here's a thought …

If you were going to give the world the greatest news of all, you probably would pick someone with some kind of status to give it. A figure who everyone would listen to.

But yet again, God surprises us! Shepherding was not considered a top career in their day. In fact, shepherds were the lowest of the low. Yet it was to them that God entrusted the news of the birth of His Son. They returned with excitement to tell others what they'd seen and heard.

May God bless you and your family with the same good news this Christmas.

'The shepherds returned, glorifying and praising God for all the things they had heard and seen, which were just as they had been told.' (Luke 2:20)

Week 15

Star stuff

Attention grabber

Wiggle your fingers
Pat your knees
Fold your arms
And look at me!

Puppet intro

[Puppet's name], I have a present for you! Would you like it?

Puppet nods, very excitedly.

OK, here it is!

Pull a fun object out from behind your back.

Do you like it?

Puppet nods, very excitedly again, and gives you a hug.

Oh good!

Our story today is about some more visitors who came to see baby Jesus and give Him some presents.

Story time

Some wise men saw a great big star. **Point up and say, 'Wow!'**

They followed the star **walk on the spot** and it led them to Mary, Joseph and baby Jesus! **Wave and say, 'Hello!'**

The wise men bowed down and worshipped Jesus. **Bow down on one knee.**

They gave Him very special presents. **Mimic holding up a present.**

That's the end of the story. Shall we do it again so you can all join in with the actions?

Repeat the story.

This story is found in Matthew 2:1–11

Things to make and do

You will need:

A star-shaped template
A4 card (white or colour)
Scissors
Glitter
Glue
Crayons
Hole punch
Ribbon

Before the group starts use the template, scissors and card to cut out card stars. Hole punch one hole onto one of the sides of the star and tie a short piece of ribbon through it so that the star can be hung up.

During the group give out the card stars, along with crayons, glitter and glue. Encourage the children to decorate their star. When they have finished, suggest that they take it home to remind them of the star that led the wise men to Jesus.

Star stuff

Your child heard this story today ...

Some wise men saw a great big star. They followed the star and it led them to Mary, Joseph and baby Jesus! The wise men bowed down and worshipped Jesus. They gave Him very special presents.

This story is found in Matthew 2:1–11

Here's a thought ...

Did you know that we are all carbon-based life forms, and that carbon itself is made at the heart of stars? In other words, we are made out of stars!

So we can see this old story of the wise men in a new way – star stuff follow a star to meet the Star-maker! No wonder they were overjoyed when they met Jesus, and no wonder they worshipped Him. We are all on our own journey, like those wise men were long ago. Where are you on your journey and where are you headed to?

'Do not detain me, now that the LORD has granted success to my journey. Send me on my way so I may go to my master.' (Genesis 24:56)

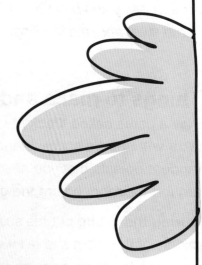

Week 16

Packing nightmare

Attention grabber

Wiggle your fingers
Pat your knees
Fold your arms
And look at me!

Puppet intro

What's that, [puppet's name]?

Puppet whispers in your ear.

You want to know how fast I can run, do you? Well, let's see!

Run slowly on the spot.

Is this fast enough?

Puppet shakes its head.

OK, OK, how about this?

Run as fast as you can on the spot.

Puppet nods, very excitedly.

Today's story is about when Joseph, Mary and baby Jesus had to run away from a nasty king.

Story time

Soon after Jesus was born in the stable, and the shepherds and wise men had gone back home, Joseph had a dream. **Put your hands under your head to mimic sleeping.**

An angel came to see him and said, 'DANGER!' **Put your palms out as if to say stop.**

King Herod wanted to hurt Jesus and any other baby boys too. **Sad face.**

He was scared that Jesus was going to be king instead of him. **Mimic putting a crown on your head.**

So Joseph got up in the night, packed the donkey and off he went with Jesus and Mary. **Walk on the spot.**

They stayed safe in Egypt until King Herod was no longer a problem. **Wipe forehead and say, 'Phew!'**

That's the end of the story. Shall we do it again so you can all join in with the actions?

Repeat the story.

This story is found in Matthew 2:13–21

Things to make and do

Play a game called 'Pack my Suitcase'. (**You will need** a suitcase and some random objects that you need to place around the room before the group starts.)

During the group put the suitcase in the middle of the room and tell the children that you need their help packing for a holiday! You are going to call out what objects you need one at a time (the ones you've placed around the room) and they need to find them and put them in the suitcase. Play until all the objects are in the suitcase. If you like you could ask each child to find you one object. At the end, tell the children that God goes with us wherever we go, just as He did when Mary and Joseph had to pack up their things and rush off to Egypt.

Packing nightmare

EGYPT

Your child heard this story today ...

Soon after Jesus was born in the stable, and the shepherds and wise men had gone back home, Joseph had a dream. An angel came to see him and said, 'DANGER!' King Herod wanted to hurt Jesus and any other baby boys too. He was scared that Jesus was going to be king instead of him. So Joseph got up in the night, packed the donkey and off he went with Jesus and Mary. They stayed safe in Egypt until King Herod was no longer a problem.

Here's a thought ...

Packing last minute for a journey or holiday can be a nightmare! And Mary and Joseph had to pack because of one! Joseph's dream had revealed a potentially devastating situation but thankfully they had been given the chance to evade it. We can only imagine how frightened and anxious they were. One day they were experiencing the joy of a new baby, the next, their world was turned upside down.

But that can happen, can't it? One day everything is fine, the next – nightmare. Yet in the face of this, God can be the constant in our lives as He was for Mary and Joseph. It's not that God took away the threat of Herod, but He was with them in it. Today this can be our experience if we allow God to be part of our lives.

'We have this hope as an anchor for the soul, firm and secure.' (Hebrews 6:19)

Week 17

Baby talk

Attention grabber

Wiggle your fingers
Pat your knees
Fold your arms
And look at me!

Puppet intro

[Puppet's name], have you ever seen something that's made you say, 'Wow'?

Puppet nods and whispers in your ear.

Fireworks! Oh yes, they are wonderful, aren't they? Children, have you ever seen something that made you say, 'Wow'?

Wait for children to respond.

Brilliant! When people saw Jesus, they often said or thought, 'Wow!'

Today our story is about two people who did just that when they met baby Jesus.

Story time

Jesus was eight days old and it was time for Him to go to God's house, the Temple.

Make a roof shape with your hands, over your head.

When Mary, Joseph and Jesus got there, they met an old man called Simeon and an old lady called Anna. **Wave and say, 'Hello!'**

Simeon wanted to hold the baby. **Mimic holding a baby.**

When Simeon and Anna looked at baby Jesus, they were surprised! **Pull a surprised face and say, 'Oh!'**

'This is a special baby,' they said. 'He is from God!' **Point up and say, 'Wow!'**

That's the end of the story. Shall we do it again so you can all join in with the actions?

Repeat the story.

This story is found in Luke 2:21–38

Things to make and do

You will need:
Simeon and Anna colouring-in sheet
Crayons

Before the group starts search the internet for colouring-in sheets of Simeon and Anna looking at baby Jesus. Download your preferred one and print out copies.

During the group hand out the sheets and crayons, and encourage the children to colour them in. When they have finished, suggest that they take their picture home so that they will be reminded of how happy people are when they meet Jesus.

Baby talk

So goo-goo!

Your child heard this story today ...

Jesus was eight days old and it was time for Him to go to God's house, the Temple. When Mary, Joseph and Jesus got there, they met an old man called Simeon and an old lady called Anna. Simeon wanted to hold the baby. When Simeon and Anna looked at baby Jesus, they were surprised! 'This is a special baby,' they said. 'He is from God!'

This story is found in Luke 2:21–38

Here's a thought ...

Baby talk can make us go goo-goo! No matter how 'serious' or 'sophisticated' we may feel, we can't help but try anything to get a baby to respond to us – even talking absolute gibberish and pulling the silliest of faces!

Today, we heard about Simeon and Anna, two older people who, when meeting the baby Jesus, actually respond to *Him*! They must have seen a lot of babies in their time, and every baby is special, yet, they sensed that this child was uniquely different.

If we open up and give Jesus the chance to come into our lives, our response will be the same – wonder, excitement and thanks!

Jesus said, 'I have come that they may have life, and have it to the full.' (John 10:10)

Week 18

Where are you?

Attention grabber

Wiggle your fingers
Pat your knees
Fold your arms
And look at me!

Puppet intro

Puppet wears necklace/hat.

Have you ever lost something and you had to go and look for it? Well, I have lost something and I can't find it anywhere. My [necklace/hat]! Have you seen it?!

Wait for children to respond.

[Puppet's name]! You had it all along!

Today's story is about when Jesus was a boy and He got lost.

Story time

Jesus went with Mary and Joseph to Jerusalem for their holiday. Lots of other people went too. On the way home Mary said, 'Where's Jesus?' **Put hands out in a questioning pose.**

Joseph didn't know. So they looked everywhere. **Search high and low.**

They ran back to Jerusalem and back to the church. **Run on the spot.**

There Jesus was talking to all the men about God! **Mimic chatting with your hands.**

They were so pleased to find Him. **Clap and say, 'Hooray!'**

That's the end of the story. Shall we do it again so you can all join in with the actions?

Repeat the story.

This story is found in Luke 2:41–50

Things to make and do

Play a game called 'Where is Jesus?' (**You will need** to download, print and cut out pictures of a young Jesus. Place them all around the room before the group starts.)

During the group show the children one of the pictures and ask them to help you find the others. If you like, you could ask them to find one each, then when they all have one, ask them to keep searching until they are all found. At the end, tell the children that just as they were looking for Jesus, God is looking for us because He wants to be our Friend.

where are you?

Your child heard this story today …

Jesus went with Mary and Joseph to Jerusalem for their holiday. Lots of other people went too. On the way home Mary said, 'Where's Jesus?' Joseph didn't know. So they looked everywhere. They ran back to Jerusalem and back to the church. There Jesus was talking to all the men about God! They were so pleased to find Him.

This story is found in Luke 2:41–50

Here's a thought …

It's a parent's worst fear. One moment your child is there with you, the next you can't find them anywhere. You call, they hear your voice and answer – relief!

Did you know that God had a similar experience in the Garden of Eden? When Adam and Eve did something wrong they hid from Him. He, like any parent, went to find them. 'Where are you?' He asked. Actually, it wasn't that He didn't know where they were (after all, He is God!), it was that He wanted them to choose to respond to His call.

God is still calling 'Where are you?' today. He is asking that question to all of us. So are we going to respond, or are we going to stay where we are?

'the LORD God called to the man, "Where are you?"' (Genesis 3:9)

© Dot to Tot

Week 19

Nice to meet you

Attention grabber

Wiggle your fingers
Pat your knees
Fold your arms
And look at me!

Puppet intro

Me and [puppet's name] are very good friends! We like to tell jokes.

Puppet whispers in your ear. Haha! And secrets.

Whisper in puppet's ear and puppet acts surprised.

Today's story is about Jesus choosing some people to be His friends.

Story time

Jesus was friends with Andrew. **Shake hands with someone.**

Andrew told his brother Simon about Jesus. **Cup your hands around your mouth and shout, 'Come and see!'**

Simon became Jesus' friend too. **Shake hands with someone else.**

They told Philip about Jesus. **Cup your hands around your mouth and shout, 'Come and see!'**

Philip became Jesus' friend too. **Shake someone else's hand.**

Philip told Nathanael about Jesus. **Cup your hands around your mouth and shout, 'Come and see!'**

Nathanael became Jesus' friend too. **Shake someone else's hand.**

That's the end of the story. Shall we do it again so you can all join in with the actions?

Repeat the story.

This story is found in John 1:40–49

Things to make and do

You will need:
Friends colouring-in sheets
Crayons

Before the group starts search the internet for colouring-in sheets with the words 'Jesus' and 'Friend'. Download your preferred one and print out copies.

During the group hand out the sheets and crayons. Encourage the children to colour in their sheet and when they have finished, suggest that they take it home to remind them that Jesus is their Friend.

Nice to meet you

Your child heard this story today ...

Jesus was friends with Andrew. Andrew told his brother Simon about Jesus. Simon became Jesus' friend too. They told Philip about Jesus. Philip became Jesus' friend too. Philip told Nathanael about Jesus. Nathanael became Jesus' friend too.

This story is found in John 1:40–49

Here's a thought ...

You see them from across the room. Everything seems to fade into the background and somehow you experience it all in slow motion ... It's the basis of many a romantic novel or film – the moment when you meet 'the one'. Sometimes this conviction stays with us, but other times we realise we have been badly mistaken!

Andrew was not mistaken. This wasn't a romantic love – it was much, much more than that. He had found the One who makes sense of life! At first it was a feeling for Andrew, call it intuition f you like, but later he came to realise that he was right. Everything pointed to it – Jesus was the One. The One who came to earth for them, the One who will save them, the One who will be with them always and will never let them down.

'Then Nathanael declared, "Rabbi, you are the Son of God; you are the king of Israel."'
(1 John 49)

Week 20

I hope so

Attention grabber

Wiggle your fingers
Pat your knees
Fold your arms
And look at me!

Puppet intro

Why are you so happy,
[puppet's name]?

Puppet whispers in your ear.

Oh, that's a very good reason.
[Puppet's name] is happy
because God loves [her/him]!
God loves you too.

*Today's story is about
something Jesus' friend,
Peter, said in the Bible.*

Story time

This is what Peter wrote in the Bible about what we should do.

Be nice to everyone you meet. **Smile and say, 'Hello!'**

Love others like God loves you. **Wrap your arms around yourself.**

If anyone is nasty to you **pull an angry face,** be nice back **smile.**

If anyone asks you why you are like that, tell them it is because God loves you!

Clap and say, 'Hooray!'

That's the end of the story. Shall we do it again so you can all join in with the actions?

Repeat the story.

This story is found in 1 Peter 3:8–9,15

Things to make and do

Play 'Musical Statues'. (**You will need** party music and some form of music player and speaker.)

During the group tell the children that when they hear the music it's time to dance! But when the music stops they need to freeze and be as still as they can until the music starts again. If you like, you can call children out if they move when the music has stopped until there is one winner (however this might not work with this age group!). At the end, ask the children if they felt happy when they were dancing. Remind them that Jesus makes us happy and our friends will notice when we're happy too!

I hope so

Your child heard this story today ...

This is what Peter wrote in the Bible about what we should do. Be nice to everyone you meet. Love others like God loves you. If anyone is nasty to you, be nice back. If anyone asks you why you are like that, tell them it is because God loves you!

This story is found in 1 Peter 3:8–9,15

Here's a thought ...

If we are asked what 'hope' means today, we would probably say: 'I hope it doesn't rain' or 'I hope things will turn out OK.' Peter wrote his book with a big hope in mind. He was encouraging us to live well because of the hope God offers us. When Christians talk of hope they mean to 'expect with confidence'. We expect with confidence that God will put all things right.

God has already begun this by putting things right in us. For are start, He helps us to love those who don't love us. You see, God is working in us and through us right now to bring about His perfect plan. So we can 'live in hope' – living out hope today and also waiting for it tomorrow.

'be prepared to give an answer to everyone who asks you to give the reason for the hope that you have.' (1 Peter 3:15)

Week 21

Always with you

Attention grabber

Wiggle your fingers
Pat your knees
Fold your arms
And look at me!

Puppet intro

[Puppet's name] was worried last week because [he/she] was left outside a shop, all alone! [She/He] didn't like it very much, did you?

Puppet shakes head.

Have you ever been all alone? You know, you never need to feel lonely because God is always with us!

Today's story is about how God cared for someone who was lonely.

Story time

Elijah was walking by himself. **Walk on the spot.**

He was all alone and he didn't have any food. **Rub tummy.**

He didn't even have anywhere to sleep! **Mimic a big yawn.**

So God sent an angel to talk to him and look after him. **Wrap your arms around yourself.**

God cared for Elijah and He cares for us too. **Clap and say, 'Hooray!'**

That's the end of the story. Shall we do it again so you can all join in with the actions?

Repeat the story.

This story is found in 1 Kings 19:3–9

Things to make and do

You will need:
Long strips of paper
Scissors
Crayons
Glitter, fabric, googly eyes, glue (optional)

Before the group starts fold the strips of paper like an accordion to make a rectangle (picture instructions can be found on the internet). Draw the outline of a person onto the rectangle, making sure the head, hands and feet touch all the edges. Now cut the person out, not cutting the folds where the hands and feet touch them as this will break the chain.

During the group hand out the people paper chains, crayons and optional extra decorations. Encourage the children to decorate their people paper chain. When they have finished, suggest that they take it home so that it will remind them that we don't ever need to feel lonely because God is with us.

Always with you

Your child heard this story today ...

Elijah was walking by himself. He was all alone and he didn't have any food. He didn't even have anywhere to sleep! So God sent an angel to talk to him and look after him. God cared for Elijah and He cares for us too.

This story is found in 1 Kings 19:3–9

Here's a thought ...

Sometimes we think the rich and famous don't have the same problems we do. But it's true that 'money can't buy you love' – or friends either! The beautiful and successful actress Anne Hathaway has said that what worries her most in life is loneliness.

In Genesis, God says that it's not good for us to be alone – that's why He made Eve as well as Adam; that's why God Himself is three Persons in one (Father, Son and Holy Spirit)!

Elijah felt alone, but he wasn't. We can *feel* alone, but we are not. God knows of our real need for relationships with others, but He also knows our deeper need for relationship with Him. And He is the One who will never, ever leave us.

'Never will I leave you; never will I forsake you.' (Hebrews 13:5)

Week 22 Mother's Day

Love you, Mum

Attention grabber

Wiggle your fingers
Pat your knees
Fold your arms
And look at me!

Puppet intro

[Puppet's name], look [baby doll's name]'s back. I am pretending to be a mummy. What do mummies do, children? Do they look after the baby?

Wait for children to respond.

Do mummies love their children?

Wait for children to respond.

When Jesus was a baby His mummy looked after Him. When He was a grown-up man He looked after her.

Today's story is about Jesus and His mum, Mary.

Story time

Jesus knew He was going away and He wanted someone to look after His mum.

Search 'high' and 'low'.

He said to His friend, John, 'Please look after my mum for me when I have gone away.'

Mimic pleading.

John was happy to look after Mary. **Thumbs up.**

Jesus loved His mum even when He was grown-up. We love our mummies too! **Wrap your arms around yourself.**

That's the end of the story. Shall we do it again so you can all join in with the actions?

Repeat the story.

This story is found in John 19:25–27

Things to make and do

You will need:

Blank cards
Blank envelopes (optional)
Crayons
Glitter, pens, tissue paper, glue (optional)

Before the group starts make a Mother's Day card as an example, using the material you will be giving the children.

During the group show the children your example and then give out the blank cards and materials. Encourage the children to decorate their cards for their mums (or carer or grandmother). Help the children write a message in their card too. At the end, encourage the children to give the cards to their mums to show they love them, just as Jesus loved His.

Love you, Mum

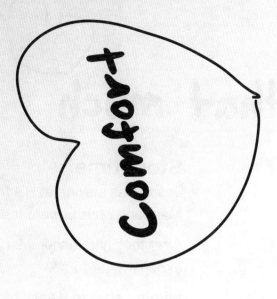

Comfort

Your child heard this story today ...

Jesus knew He was going away and He wanted someone to look after His mum. He said to His friend, John, 'Please look after my mum for me when I have gone away.' John was happy to look after Mary. Jesus loved His mum even when He was grown-up. We love our mummies too!

This story is found in John 19:25–27

Here's a thought ...

When and if we think of God, we most likely think of Him as male. After all, we say "He" and also, two Persons of the Trinity are called Father and Son. Yet in Genesis it says that God created us in His image, *both* men and women.

Jesus showed motherly care for His mum at a difficult point in His life. He wanted to comfort and look after her; in some way returning the love and comfort He received as a child.

Isaiah, a man in the Bible, says that God has a heart for us like a mother has for her child, a heart that wants to comfort us. He is ready to hold us, but He waits to be asked.

'As a mother comforts her child, so will I comfort you' (Isaiah 66:13)

Week 23

Worth that much

Attention grabber

Wiggle your fingers
Pat your knees
Fold your arms
And look at me!

Puppet intro

[Puppet's name] is wearing perfume today.

Smell puppet.

Oh, you smell very nice!

Today's story is about how someone brought some perfume for Jesus.

Story time

Jesus was staying at His friend Lazarus' house. Mary and Martha were there too.

After they had dinner, Mary brought out a big jar of expensive perfume.

Mimic carrying a very big jar.

Mary poured the perfume all over Jesus' feet!
Mimic pouring the jar.

How lovely! **Take a big breath in through your nose.**

Some people said it was a waste of money. **Pull an angry face.**

But Jesus liked it very much. 'Well done, Mary!' He said.

That's the end of the story. Shall we do it again so you can all join in with the actions?

Repeat the story.

This story is found in John 12:1–7

Things to make and do

Play a game called 'What's that Lovely Smell?' (**You will need** a blindfold and five tubs. Put separately in the tubs: a dollop of chocolate spread, tomato ketchup, an orange peel, a lemon and a cut up banana.)

During the group let the children take it in turns to put on the blindfold (or close their eyes), smell each tub and try to guess what the smell is. At the end remind the children of the perfume story and that it shows us just how special Jesus is.

Worth that much

Your child heard this story today ...

Jesus was staying at His friend Lazarus' house. Mary and Martha were there too. After they had dinner, Mary brought out a big jar of expensive perfume. Mary poured the perfume all over Jesus' feet! How lovely! Some people said it was a waste of money. But Jesus liked it very much. 'Well done, Mary!' He said.

This story is found in John 12:1–7

Here's a thought ...

The last drops of an expensive perfume can be precious. For Mary, this perfume was worth more than a year's wages. Now that's expensive! She lavished it all on Jesus' feet as a profound act of selfless worship. Why? She knew that Jesus was more than just any man. So this was an act of adoration. She wanted to give Him something precious, something that cost her dearly. She could do this because she knew her future was secure with Him. He was worth it.

Are you holding back from following Jesus because you're worried about what it will cost you? Could you believe that the free gift Jesus offers you is worth it?

'For the wages of sin is death, but the gift of God is eternal life in Christ Jesus our Lord.' (Romans 6:23)

Week 24 Palm Sunday

Starstruck

Attention grabber

Wiggle your fingers
Pat your knees
Fold your arms
And look at me!

Puppet intro

Puppet waves.

What are you doing,
[puppet's name]?

Puppet whispers in your ear.

You're practising your waving?
What a fun idea. Shall we all
practise waving?

Wave at the children.

*Our story today is about when
lots of people came out to
wave at Jesus.*

Story time

Jesus was going to the big city, Jerusalem. When He
was nearly there, He asked His disciples to get Him a
donkey to ride on. They found one and Jesus got on.

Mimic getting onto a donkey and riding along.

When Jesus arrived in Jerusalem, everyone came
out into the street to see Him. **Run on the spot
and point.**

They got palm branches to wave and they called out
'Hosanna!', which means: Hooray! Jesus is King!

Mimic waving a palm branch and say, 'Hooray!'

That's the end of the story. Shall we do it again so
you can all join in with the actions?

Repeat the story.

This story is found in John 12:12–16

Things to make and do

You will need:
Large sheets of green card
Pairs of children's scissors
Short bamboo sticks or dowel rods
Sticky or masking tape

Before the group starts draw a palm leaf
outline on each of the sheets of card.

During the group hand out the scissors and
sheets with outlines on and encourage the

children to cut out their leaves (make sure
you have a few assistants to help them).
Once they have finished, use the tape to
attach the sticks or rods to the back of the
leaves to make the stem. When every child
has a finished palm leaf, gather the children
together and encourage them to wave their
leaves and shout 'Hosanna', just like people
did for Jesus in the story.

Starstruck

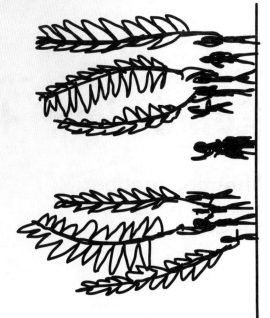

Your child heard this story today ...

Jesus was going to the big city, Jerusalem. When He was nearly there, He asked His disciples to get Him a donkey to ride on. They found one and Jesus got on. When Jesus arrived in Jerusalem, everyone came out into the street to see Him. They got palm branches to wave and they called out 'Hosanna!', which means: Hooray! Jesus is King!

This story is found in John 12:12–16

Here's a thought ...

Have you ever seen a famous face in real life? It can be exciting, surreal even! You can get caught up in it all – maybe not turning into a screaming teenager, but you might feel strangely elated!

Sometimes we can experience this at church. We sense something good, something that's beyond us, attractive, and we want to be a part of it. We might sing a song or say a prayer in response.

Unlike our moments with celebrities, it doesn't need to be so fleeting. It can be the beginning of something taking root, bringing deeper meaning to our lives. God is not confined to buildings, or to one place at one time. You can experience His presence anytime, anywhere.

'For the LORD your God is God of gods and Lord of lords, the great God, mighty and awesome' (Deuteronomy 10:17)

Week 25

Remember this

Attention grabber

Wiggle your fingers
Pat your knees
Fold your arms
And look at me!

Puppet intro

Puppet holds an Easter egg.

What is [puppet's name] holding?

Wait for children to respond.

That's right, it's an Easter egg!
An Easter egg reminds us about
Easter and the Easter story in the
Bible. Sometimes we have special
food to remind us of special times.

**If appropriate, hand out
pieces of the Easter egg to
introduce children to the idea
of Jesus sharing His last meal
with friends.**

*Today our story is about a
special meal Jesus shared with
His friends.*

Story time

Jesus' friends made a special meal. **Mimic mixing
in a bowl.**

Jesus and His friends sat down at the table.
Mimic pulling out a chair.

Jesus shared the food between His friends.
Mimic passing food out.

Jesus was going away. **Wave.**

Jesus said His friends would think of Him every time
they shared food like this. **Tap the side of your head.**

That's the end of the story. Shall we do it again so
you can all join in with the actions?

Repeat the story.

This story is found in Luke 22:14–20

Things to make and do

You will need:
Last Supper colouring-in sheets
Crayons

Before the group starts search the
internet for colouring-in sheets of the Last
Supper. Download your preferred one and
print out copies.

During the group hand out the sheets and
crayons. Encourage the children to colour
in their sheet and when they have finished,
suggest that they take it home to remind
them of the special meal Jesus had with
His friends.

Remember this

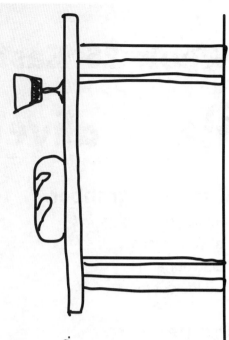

Your child heard this story today ...

Jesus' friends made a special meal. Jesus and His friends sat down at the table. Jesus shared the food between His friends. Jesus was going away. Jesus said His friends would think of Him every time they shared food like this.

This story is found in Luke 22:14–20

Here's a thought ...

It can be odd for us when we first see a Communion service. We may very well ask, *'What* exactly is going on?' What's the deal with the little piece of bread or wafer? And what about the wine (or more often, fruit juice!)?

The bread and wine are reminders and there is something special that happens when we remember what Jesus did for us, when we know that He is with us and when we look forward to seeing Him face to face one day. We are somehow fed, with a sip of wine and a bit of bread, deep inside. Eat up.

'Then Jesus declared, "I am the bread of life. Whoever comes to me will never go hungry, and whoever believes in me will never be thirsty."' (John 6:35)

Week 26 Easter

He is alive!

Attention grabber

Wiggle your fingers
Pat your knees
Fold your arms
And look at me!

Puppet intro

Puppet holds a toy rabbit.

What have you got there,
[puppet's name]?

Puppet lifts the rabbit up.

A rabbit! What do rabbits do,
children?

Wait for children to respond.

They jump and bounce,
don't they?

Let's all have a go at bouncing.

Jump up and down.

*Today our story is about the first
Easter – when Jesus bounced
back to life!*

Story time

Jesus' friends were sad. **Pull a very sad
face.** They didn't think they were going to see
Him anymore.

Mary was one of the people looking for Jesus.
Mimic searching high and low.

She saw an angel. **Flap your arms like wings.**

And then she saw Jesus! **Point in front of you.**

He was alive!

Jump up and say, 'Hooray!'

That was the first Easter.

That's the end of the story. Shall we do it again so
you can all join in with the actions?

Repeat the story.

This story is found in John 20:1–18

Things to make and do

Play 'Pass the Parcel'. (**You will need** to
prepare the parcel before the group starts
and you will need party music and some
form of music player and speaker. You could
use small Easter eggs as the prizes between
each sheet of wrapping paper.)

During the group ask the children to sit
in a circle. Tell them that when they hear
the music it's time to pass the parcel to the
child on their left. When the music stops,
whoever is holding the parcel gets to open
one layer and take the prize. Once you
think the children understand the game,
give the parcel to a child to start, and stop
and start the music, playing until every
child has won a prize. At the end, remind
the children that Easter is a very happy
time because of Jesus!

He is alive!

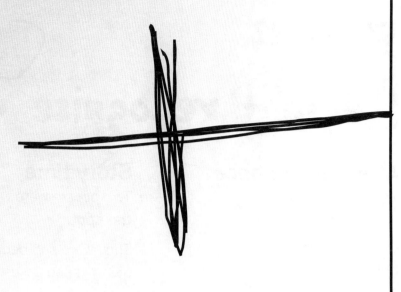

Your child heard this story today …

Jesus' friends were sad. They didn't think they were going to see Him anymore. Mary was one of the people looking for Jesus. She saw an angel. And then she saw Jesus! He was alive! That was the first Easter.

This story is found in John 20:1–18

Here's a thought …

You may not know this but when the New Testament was written, before the age of equality, a woman's evidence was not admissible in court. And yet who does the Bible say was the first witness of the resurrection of Jesus? Mary.

The Bible records that over 500 people saw the risen Jesus. He appeared in front of friends and He appeared in front of skeptics. So why was Mary first? Simply because she was there first! She was searching diligently for Her Saviour. And God promises that those who search for Him will find Him.

'You will seek me and find me when you seek me with all your heart.' (Jeremiah 29:13)

Week 27

I didn't recognise you

Attention grabber

Wiggle your fingers
Pat your knees
Fold your arms
And look at me!

Puppet intro

Puppet is wearing a wig and glasses.

Who's this, children?

Wait for children to respond.

Ah, you're not fooled by [his/her] disguise! It's [puppet's name]!

Today's story is about two people who didn't recognise someone very important.

Story time

Two people were walking down the road. **Walk on the spot.**

They were sad because they didn't think they were going to see Jesus anymore. **Pull a sad face.**

A man joined in walking with them. **Walk on the spot again.**

But they didn't know who it was. When they got to their house they invited the stranger in. **Beckon.**

When they had tea together they saw it was Jesus! **Look surprised and say, 'Wow!'**

He was back with them! What a lovely surprise!

That's the end of the story. Shall we do it again so you can all join in with the actions?

Repeat the story.

This story is found in Luke 24:13–35

Things to make and do

Play 'Blind Man's Bluff'. (**You will need a blindfold.**)

During the group ask the children to gather together and explain that one child will be blindfolded and they will walk around until they catch another child, then that child will put on the blindfold and so on. Once you think the children understand the game, ask who would like to go first then help them put the blindfold on. If the 'blind man' is finding it hard to catch someone, ask the other children to stand still. Play until every child who would like a go has gone. At the end, remind the children of today's story and that we can 'open our eyes' to Jesus.

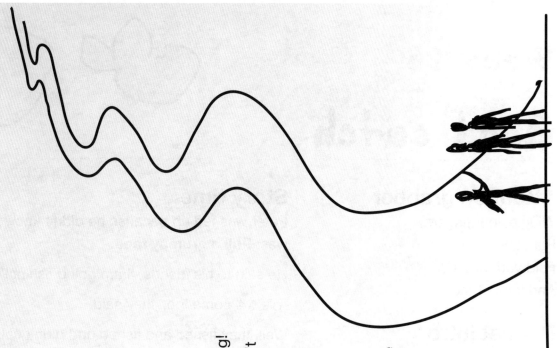

I didn't recognise you

Your child heard this story today ...

Two people were walking down the road. They were sad because they didn't think they were going to see Jesus anymore. A man joined in walking with them. But they didn't know who it was. When they got to their house they invited the stranger in. When they had tea together they saw it was Jesus! He was back with them! What a lovely surprise!

This story is found in Luke 24:13–35

Here's a thought ...

A guy was operating a roller-coaster at a theme park, and as he was securing a passenger into his seat he recognised the passenger's face. 'I know you,' he said, 'but I can't remember your name.'

Without blinking, the passenger said, 'My name is Harry.' It was then the guy noticed the Royal security guards watching!

It seems strange that Jesus' friends didn't recognise Him at first. Perhaps Jesus prevented them from knowing or maybe they were just so blind from their grief and hopelessness.

Sometimes we don't recognise that God is with us. It's only when we look back that we see how He has been walking alongside us all along.

'I am with you and will watch over you wherever you go' (Genesis 28:15)

Week 28

Good catch

Attention grabber

Wiggle your fingers
Pat your knees
Fold your arms
And look at me!

Puppet intro

Puppet has a fish.

[Puppet's name], what's that you've got? Oh, it's a fish!

Do you know where fish come from, children?

Wait for children to respond.

They come from the sea! Fishermen and women catch them for us! Some of Jesus' friends were fishermen.

Today's story is about how they had a lovely surprise when they went fishing one day.

Story time

Peter was fed up because he didn't know where Jesus was. **Pull a grumpy face.**

He said to his friends, 'I am going fishing!'

'We will come too,' they said.

Well, they fished and fished and didn't catch a thing. **Thumbs down.**

Then they saw someone on the beach. **Point.**

The man on the beach said, 'Try fishing on the other side of the boat.'

So they did and caught loads! **Thumbs up.**

Who was it on the beach? Peter knew! He shouted, 'It's JESUS!'

They raced back to share the fish with Him. **Run on the spot.**

That's the end of the story. Shall we do it again so you can all join in with the actions?

Repeat the story.

This story is found in John 21:1–6

Things to make and do

You will need:
A4 card (colour or white)
Crayons
Glitter, tissue paper, stickers, googly eyes, glue (optional)
A hole punch
Wool or ribbon

Before the group starts draw simple fish shapes on the card and cut out. Hole punch a hole near the mouths of the fish and tie a piece of ribbon or wool through so that they can be hung up.

During the group give the children a fish each and pass out the crayons and extra materials if desired. Encourage the children to decorate their fish. At the end, remind the children that Jesus' friends were fishermen and Jesus performed a miracle, helping them catch a lot of fish! And Jesus looks after us too!

Good catch

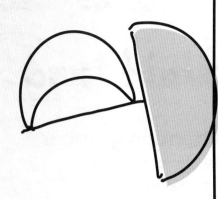

Your child heard this story today ...

Peter was fed up because he didn't know where Jesus was. He said to his friends, 'I am going fishing!'

'We will come too,' they said.

Well, they fished and fished and didn't catch a thing. Then they saw someone on the beach. The man on the beach said, 'Try fishing on the other side of the boat.'

So they did and caught loads! Who was it on the beach? Peter knew! He shouted, 'It's JESUS!'

They raced back to share the fish with Him.

This story is found in John 21:1–6

Here's a thought ...

If fishing teaches us one thing, it's patience! For Peter, it had been a bad night for fish. Actually, it had been a terrible time in general. Jesus had just been crucified, and with Jesus died all Peter's hopes.

But then something happened. Peter recognised it was more than luck when a figure in the morning light directed their nets so that they filled to bursting. It was Jesus.

When they arrived on the beach, Jesus had prepared breakfast for them, perhaps to show He was fully alive. If that was and is true, it changes everything. It rewrites the possibilities in our own life, and life after death.

'if you declare with your mouth, "Jesus is Lord," and believe in your heart that God raised him from the dead, you will be saved.'
(Romans 10:9)

Week 29 Ascension
Wait and see

Attention grabber

Wiggle your fingers
Pat your knees
Fold your arms
And look at me!

Puppet intro

Puppet has a bag.

[Puppet name], why have you got a packed bag? Are you going away?

Puppet whispers in your ear.

You're going on holiday! Oh, that's lovely. But I will miss you though.

Hug puppet.

Today's story is about when Jesus went back into heaven.

Story time

It was time for Jesus to go back to heaven to be with His Father.

Jesus' friends didn't want Him to go.
Mimic sobbing.

Jesus said, 'Don't be worried, because I will make you strong.' **Mimic strong arms.**

'You must go and tell everyone about me and tell them that God loves them.' **Wrap your arms around yourself.**

Then a cloud came down and hid Jesus.
Cover your eyes.

When the cloud moved Jesus was gone!
Open eyes.

His friends were sad but they stayed together and waited to see what would happen next.

That's the end of the story. Shall we do it again so you can all join in with the actions?

Repeat the story.

This story is found in Acts 1:1–15

Things to make and do

You will need:
Jesus in clouds colouring-in sheets
Crayons
Cotton wool
Glue

Before the group starts search the internet for colouring-in sheets of Jesus going in the clouds to heaven. Download your preferred one and print out copies.

During the group hand out the sheets and crayons. Encourage the children to colour in their sheet. Then hand out the cotton wool and glue and help the children stick the wool onto the clouds to make them nice and fluffy! When they have finished, suggest that they take their picture home to remind them that Jesus went back in the clouds to heaven, but He is still always with us.

Wait and see

Your child heard this story today ...

It was time for Jesus to go back to heaven to be with His Father. Jesus' friends didn't want Him to go. Jesus said, 'Don't be worried, because I will make you strong. You must go and tell everyone about me and tell them that God loves them.' Then a cloud came down and hid Jesus. When the cloud moved Jesus was gone! His friends were sad but they stayed together and waited to see what would happen next.

This story is found in Acts 1:1–15

Here's a thought ...

In *The Hitchhiker's Guide to the Galaxy*, earth is about to be destroyed and so, naturally, all the dolphins evacuate! Their final message: 'So long and thanks for all the fish!'

For many, Jesus' disappearance is equally baffling. But He did not float off into the clouds or leave this world to its own destruction. He stepped out of our 'space' into His. He is still close, whether we can see Him or not. That's why He is able to say goodbye but also that He would always be with us.

Wouldn't it be easier to believe in Jesus if we could see Him with our own eyes? Well, of course, yes! But that is not faith. One day we will see Jesus face to face, but for now, what will we believe?

'Now faith is confidence in what we hope for and assurance about what we do not see.' (Hebrews 11:1)

Week 30 Pentecost

I've got the power

Attention grabber

Wiggle your fingers
Pat your knees
Fold your arms
And look at me!

Puppet intro

Are you good at waiting? Let's see if [puppet's name] is good at waiting.

Sit puppet on your lap. After a few seconds, the puppet starts twitching, then taps you, getting more and more angry.

Oh dear. It's hard waiting, isn't it?

Today's story is about when Jesus' friends had to wait for something.

Story time

Jesus' friends had seen Jesus go back to heaven. **Wave up at the ceiling and say, 'Bye bye.'**

Now they were waiting for something to happen. They waited ... and waited ... **Fold your arms and huff and puff.**

And then the wind began to blow. **Blow loudly and for as long as you can.**

Little flames came on their heads. **Mimic flames with your hands and put them above your head.**

It was very exciting! They knew that Jesus was giving them His power. **Punch the air!**

That's the end of the story. Shall we do it again so you can all join in with the actions?

Repeat the story.

This story is found in Acts 2:1–4

Things to make and do

Play a game called 'Earth, Wind and Fire'.

During the group gather the children together and explain that they are going to walk around the room and listen to what you call out. When you say 'Earth' they need to scrunch up into a ball. When you say 'Wind' they need to blow as loudly as they can. When you say 'Fire' they need to mimic a flickering flame with their fingers and say

'Crackle, crackle, crackle'. Play the game, alternating what you call out and reminding the children to keep walking around the room. If you like, you could call children out who were last to respond until there is one winner. At the end, remind the children of today's story of how the Holy Spirit came to earth and showed His power through wind and fire.

I've got the power

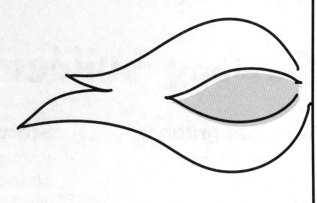

Your child heard this story today …

Jesus' friends had seen Jesus go back to heaven. Now they were waiting for something to happen. They waited … and waited … And then the wind began to blow. Little flames came on their heads. It was very exciting! They knew that Jesus was giving them His power.

This story is found in Acts 2:1–4

Here's a thought …

Don't be put off by the wind and fire. Today's story illustrates probably the most mind-blowing thing that Christians believe (after Jesus dying for us and coming back to life of course!), which is that God wants to, and can, *live in us*.

We can have the odds-defying power of God, the no-matter-what-we're-going-through peace of God, the unconditional love of God – all of it – living in us!

Just as those disciples experienced all those years ago, we can invite the Holy Spirit to come into our lives – to come and stay! There might not be any 'signs and wonders' like the wind and fire seen then, but we cannot expect to allow God in without seeing dramatic change in our lives.

'For the Spirit God gave us does not make us timid, but gives us power, love and self-discipline.' (2 Timothy 1:7)

Week 31

Cowboy builders

Attention grabber

Wiggle your fingers
Pat your knees
Fold your arms
And look at me!

Puppet intro

Puppet is holding a toy brick.

What have you got there, [puppet's name]? Oh, it's a brick! You like building, don't you?

Puppet nods enthusiastically.

Do you like building too?

Wait for children to respond.

Today's story is one Jesus told about two builders.

Story time

There were once two builders who were each building a house. **Clench your hands into fists and place one fist on top of the other. 'Build them' higher and higher by swapping them over.**

One was clever. The other one not so clever. The first one built on the sand and that house fell down when it rained! **Unclench your fists and, with flat hands, sweep your hands across your lap.**

The second one was clever and built a house on the rock. It took longer but it didn't fall down, even when the rain came. **Clench your hands into fists again and place one top of the other.**

Jesus said we must be like the clever builder.

That's the end of the story. Shall we do it again so you can all join in with the actions?

Repeat the story.

This story is found in Matthew 7:24–28

Things to make and do

Play a game called 'Tall Towers'. (**You will need** toy building bricks.)

During the group pile out the bricks onto the floor and encourage the children to build towers – as tall as they can! If the towers fall down, encourage the children to start again. At the end, tell the children that our lives can be like good, strong, tall buildings when we listen to Jesus!

Cowboy builders

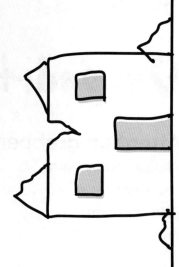

Your child heard this story today ...

There were once two builders who were each building a house. One was clever. The other one not so clever. The first one built on the sand and that house fell down when it rained! The second one was clever and built a house on the rock. It took longer but it didn't fall down, even when the rain came. Jesus said we must be like the clever builder.

This story is found in Matthew 7:24–28

Here's a thought ...

Have you ever realised, about one week in, that the builder who you are paying to do a job should have spurs and a ten gallon hat? If not you, maybe you have heard the stories.

The trouble is we are good at bad building work ourselves. It's easy for us to base our lives on foundations that, when difficult times come, don't stand the test. When they fail, when they break down, we begin to see them as they really are. Like a dodgy wall or a bad ceiling, life can come crashing down on our heads. Jesus encourages us to see that it's not just His words but *Him* in whom we can completely trust. A building that will stand

'everyone who hears these words of mine and puts them into practice is like a wise man who built his house on the rock.' (Matthew 7:24)

Week 32

Unconditional love

Attention grabber

Wiggle your fingers
Pat your knees
Fold your arms
And look at me!

Puppet intro

Puppet looks sad.

Children, [puppet's name] was a little bit naughty today. [He/She] took more biscuits then [he/she]'s allowed and ate them. But do you know what? That doesn't mean I love [him/her] any less. You said sorry too, didn't you?

Puppet looks up and nods.

I love you, [puppet's name].

Hug puppet.

Today's story is about how God loves us all the time, no matter what we've done.

This story is found in Ephesians 2:1–10

Story time

After Jesus had gone back to heaven, a man called Paul wrote to people to tell them that God loved them. He said that God loves us when we're happy. **Pull a happy face.**

And He loves us when we're sad. **Pull a sad face.**

God loves us when we're good. **Fold arms and look proud.**

And He loves us when we're not so good. **Blow a raspberry.**

God loves us just as we are. And God sent Jesus to show us how to live! **Jump up and say, 'Hooray!'**

That's the end of the story. Shall we do it again so you can all join in with the actions?

Repeat the story.

Things to make and do

You will need:

'God loves me' colouring-in sheets
Crayons

Before the group starts search the internet for colouring-in sheets with the words 'God loves me'. Download your preferred one and print out copies.

During the group hand out the sheets and crayons. Encourage the children to colour in their sheet. When they have finished, suggest that they take it home to remind them that God really does love them – all the time!

Unconditional love

Your child heard this story today …

After Jesus had gone back to heaven, a man called Paul wrote to people to tell them that God loved them. He said that God loves us when we're happy. And He loves us when we're sad. God loves us when we're good. And He loves us when we're not so good. God loves us just as we are. And God sent Jesus to show us how to live!

This story is found in Ephesians 2:1–10

Here's a thought …

There once was a young girl who suffered badly from travel sickness. When she arrived home from school one day to meet her dad, she ran to him and he lovingly scooped her up (in her sick-soaked clothes) and hugged her with all his might.

This story paints a picture of how our relationship with God can be. We do stuff that hurts God, we make some not-so-great decisions. Our gut-instinct might be to run and hide our mess in an effort to 'keep up appearances'. But the truth is, we get nowhere that way.

God has the power to clean up any mess we make and give us a new start. God, our loving Father, wants to embrace us, help us and love us, no matter what we have done. We just have to run to Him, not from Him.

'immense in mercy and with an incredible love, he embraced us. He took our sin-dead lives and made us alive in Christ.' (Ephesians 2:4, *The Message*)

Week 33 Father's Day

Do you know my dad?

Attention grabber

Wiggle your fingers
Pat your knees
Fold your arms
And look at me!

Puppet intro

Who loves their daddy?

Wait for children to respond.

[Puppet's name] loves [his/her] daddy too!

Puppet nods.

Some people don't have daddies and that is sad, isn't it?

But in our story today we will hear that we all have a Daddy in heaven!

Story time

Jesus was talking to His disciples one day. They asked Jesus, 'What is God like and how should we talk to Him?' **Scratch head.**

Jesus said, 'God is the best daddy in the whole world. He is *everyone's* Daddy. He loves us all so much and He doesn't have favourites!' **Wrap your arms around yourself and smile.**

Jesus' disciples were surprised. **Gasp and pull a surprised face.**

Jesus said, 'When you pray, then, you can call Him Daddy or Father. Because that is what He is!' **Clap and say, 'Hooray!'**

That's the end of the story. Shall we do it again so you can all join in with the actions?

Repeat the story.

This story is found in Matthew 6:9

Things to make and do

You will need:
Blank cards
Blank envelopes (optional)
Crayons
Glitter, pens, tissue paper, glue (optional)

Before the group starts make a Father's Day card as an example, using the material you will be giving the children.

During the group show the children your example and then give out the blank cards and materials. Encourage the children to decorate their cards for their dads (or carer or grandfather). Help the children write a message in their card too. At the end, encourage the children to give the cards to their dads to show they love them, just as their dads – and God – loves them.

Do you know my dad?

Your child heard this story today ...

Jesus was talking to His disciples one day. They asked Jesus, 'What is God like and how should we talk to Him?'

Jesus said, 'God is the best daddy in the whole world. He is *everyone's* Daddy. He loves us all so much and He doesn't have favourites!'

Jesus' disciples were surprised.

Jesus said, "When you pray, then, you can call Him Daddy or Father. Because that is what He is!'

This story is found in Matthew 6:9

Here's a thought ...

Many of us remember it from our days in the school playground. A fight breaks out between two children and then one of them uses that classic line: 'Do you know who my dad is?' Did it ever work?

Whether it did or not, it highlights just how much we need to feel protected and supported by something or someone.

Really, there is only One who can fulfil this. Our Father in heaven. He is bigger than any problems or battles we face. He is the Creator of the universe but, and this is breathtaking, Jesus actually encourages us to call Him Dad. Jesus wants us to enjoy with Him the kind of loving relationship that is beyond the scope of even the most perfect of fathers.

Do you know who *your* heavenly Dad is?

'If you, then ... know how to give good gifts to your children, how much more will your Father in heaven give good gifts to those who ask him!' (Matthew 7:11)

Week 34

Not beyond reach

Attention grabber

Wiggle your fingers
Pat your knees
Fold your arms
And look at me!

Puppet intro

How tall are you, [puppet's name]?

Hold the puppet so its feet touch the ground and put your hand on its head. Now, keeping your hand where it is, move the puppet out the way.

Quite tall! How tall am I?

Put your hand on your head then, keeping your hand where it is, step out.

A bit taller! How tall is this room?

Try to touch the ceiling, jumping up and down.

Very tall!

Our story today is about how tall, wide and big God's love is.

Story time

After Jesus had gone back to heaven, a man called Paul wrote to people to tell them that God loved them. **Mimic writing a letter.**

He said, 'God's love is sooo big! It is really high **stretch up,** wide **stretch out,** deep **reach down** and long **reach forward.** And God loves us all.'

Clap and say, 'Hooray!'

That's the end of the story. Shall we do it again so you can all join in with the actions?

Repeat the story.

This story is found in Ephesians 3:14–21

Things to make and do

You will need:
A4 card (colour or white)
Crayons

Before the group starts draw and cut different size hearts out of the card. Make some wider, some taller, some bigger and some smaller.

During the group give out the hearts so that every child has one of each size and encourage the children to colour them in. When they have finished, ask the children to hold up the small hearts, then the tall hearts, then the big hearts, then the wide hearts. Suggest that they take their hearts home to remind them that God's love for them is high, deep, long and wide!

Not beyond reach

Your child heard this story today …

After Jesus had gone back to heaven, a man called Paul wrote to people to tell them that God loved them. He said, 'God's love is sooo big! It is really high, wide, deep and long. And God loves us all.'

This story is found in Ephesians 3:14–21

Here's a thought …

What is the best view you have ever seen? The surrounding mountains from the top of Ben Nevis or all of Paris from the Eiffel Tower? How about majestic views over the Grand Canyon? Whatever it is, these sorts of sights are breathtaking, awe-inspiring, beautiful – but somehow distant and out of our reach.

Paul, writing to the Ephesians, is saying this: the love of God is breathtaking, awe-inspiring and beautiful – and yet it is not distant. Quite the contrary, it couldn't be closer! God's love reaches out to us today, in all its height, length, width and depth!

'I pray that you … may … grasp how wide and long and high and deep is the love of Christ' (Ephesians 3:17–18)

Week 35

Church, assemble!

Attention grabber

Wiggle your fingers
Pat your knees
Fold your arms
And look at me!

Puppet intro

Oh, I'm so tired!

Puppet whispers in your ear.

Why am I tired?

Puppet nods.

Well, I had to tidy up my whole house all on my own. It was exhausting!

Puppet whispers in your ear again.

Oh, you'll help me next time!

Puppet nods enthusiastically.

Oh, thank you, that would really help me out!

Our story today is about how the Bible tells us to work together.

Story time

It says in the Bible that we should all be kind and gentle to each other. **Pull a massive smile.**

God's love will bind us together. **Wrap your arms around yourself.**

We are all good at something. Some are good at running **run on the spot**, others at jumping **jump up and down**. Some are good at hopping **hop on one foot**, while others at singing **mimic singing into a microphone**.

We can be a great team when we all work together.

That's the end of the story. Shall we do it again so you can all join in with the actions?

Repeat the story.

This story is found in Ephesians 4:1–13

Things to make and do

Play a game called 'Building Factory'.
(**You will need** some toy building bricks.)

During the group ask the children to stand in a line. At one end, put a pile of building bricks. The child next to the bricks needs to pick one up and pass it to the next child in the line, who then passes it to the next and so on until the child at the end of the line has it. Then they need to place it on the floor then walk to the other end of the line (where the bricks are), picking a brick up and passing it down the line so that the new child at the end can place that brick on top. Continue until all the bricks have been passed down and the children have built a tower. At the end show the children what they have built *together*, reminding them that team work is great! Repeat the game if you like.

Church, assemble!

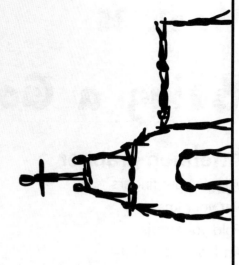

Your child heard this story today ...

It says in the Bible that we should all be kind and gentle to each other. God's love will bind us together. We are all good at something. Some are good at running, others at jumping. Some are good at hopping, while others at singing. We can be a great team when we all work together.

Here's a thought ...

We all believed it once. It's a classic misconception. We thought that the Church was the *building*. But that is not the truth! When the original word for 'church' was being translated into English, there were several options. One was 'church', another was the word 'assembly', meaning a group of people. In the Bible, the Church is the *people*. It's even called 'the Body', which gives you an idea of how Christians believe we should be completely united, as a hand is to its arm!

So when the Church, or the Body, assembles, you get all sorts of different people, different ages, different talents, all meeting with one thing in common – their desire to know and worship God. Like family, it's not always easy but it's God's love that binds this family together, making it stronger than anything we could do in our own strength!

'Be completely humble and gentle; be patient, bearing with one another in love." (Ephesians 4:2)

Week 36

Being a Good Samaritan

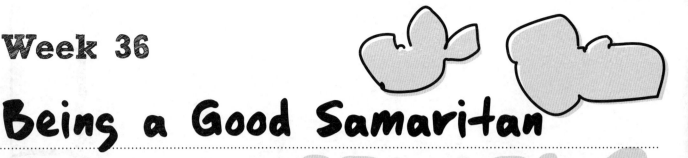

Attention grabber

Wiggle your fingers
Pat your knees
Fold your arms
And look at me!

Puppet intro

The puppet is wearing a plaster.

Children, [puppet's name] fell over today. Poor [puppet's name]. But [he/she] was very brave and someone very kind gave [him/her] a plaster. Didn't they?

Puppet nods happily.

Today's story is one Jesus told about looking after other people.

Story time

A man was walking along the road when he got hurt by some bad people. Oh dear! Who will help? **Scratch your chin.**

A priest came along. Will he help? **Shake head.** NO, too busy!

A teacher came along. Will she help? **Shake head.** NO, too busy!

Here comes someone we don't know ... He won't help, will he? **Shake head.**

Oh wait! Yes he does! **Nod head.**

He helps the poor person and takes him to the hospital.

Jesus said we should be like that and help people, no matter who they are. **Nod head.**

That's the end of the story. Shall we do it again so you can all join in with the actions?

Repeat the story.

This story is found in Luke 10:25–37

Things to make and do

Play a game called 'Pin the Plaster on the Poorly Person'. (**You will need** a large sheet of paper with a drawing of a person's sad face and bump on their head, a blindfold and pack of plasters.)

During the group stick the picture on a wall in easy reach of the children. Tell the children that they are going to take it in turns to be blindfolded and try to stick the plaster on the poorly person's bump. Play the game, helping each child to be blindfolded and giving them each a plaster with the wrapper taken off. The winner is the child who stuck their plaster nearest to the bump. At the end, remind the children of today's story and tell them that Jesus wants us to care for one another.

Being a Good Samaritan

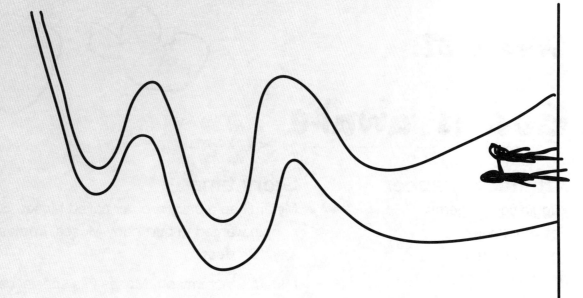

Your child heard this story today …

A man was walking along the road when he got hurt by some bad people. Oh dear! Who will help? A priest came along. Will he help? NO, too busy! A teacher came along. Will she help? NO, too busy! Here comes someone we don't know … He won't help, will he? Oh wait! Yes he does! He helps the poor person and takes him to the hospital. Jesus said we should be like that and help people, no matter who they are.

This story is found in Luke 10:25–37

Here's a thought …

The term 'good Samaritan' has fallen into general use. We may all know the work of the Samaritans helpline and when we see someone care for a stranger we say they're a 'good Samaritan'. But what we might miss if we don't know the real context of this Bible story is something pivotal – and really, the main reason for the story!

Those listening to Jesus tell this story were Jews. And Jews *hated* Samaritans! So to hear that a Jewish man had walked by his fellow Jew in desperate need, but then a Samaritan came to his rescue, must have been shocking. Jesus was making the point that our care for each other should not be determined by how much we like someone or indeed if they are like us. We are to show love because of the way God loves us.

'Jesus told him, "Go and do likewise."' (Luke 10:37)

Week 37

God is awake

Attention grabber

Wiggle your fingers
Pat your knees
Fold your arms
And look at me!

Puppet intro

[Puppet's name], we have a friend today. This is [baby doll's name]. Children, do any of you have a baby sister or brother?

Wait for children to respond.

Babies need a lot of looking after. Do you help look after them?

Wait for children to respond.

Today's story is about a special baby in the Bible. He was called Moses and he had a very good big sister.

Story time

Miriam had a baby brother called Moses. Some bad people wanted to hurt baby Moses. **Look shocked and say, 'Oh dear!'**

Miriam's mummy put Moses in a special basket. **Cup hands.**

She hid the basket in the river reeds. **Mimic hiding something.**

Miriam stayed with Moses to watch over him and make sure he was safe. **Mimic looking through binoculars.**

Miriam was a good big sister. She was God's helper! **Clap.**

That's the end of the story. Shall we do it again so you can all join in with the actions?

Repeat the story.

This story is found in Exodus 2:1–10

Things to make and do

You will need:
Miriam and Moses colouring-in sheets
Crayons

Before the group starts search the internet for colouring-in sheets of Miriam putting baby Moses into a basket and into the water. Download your preferred one and print out copies.

During the group hand out the sheets and crayons. Encourage the children to colour in their sheet. When they have finished, suggest that they take it home to remind them that God watches over us, like Miriam watched over Moses.

God is awake

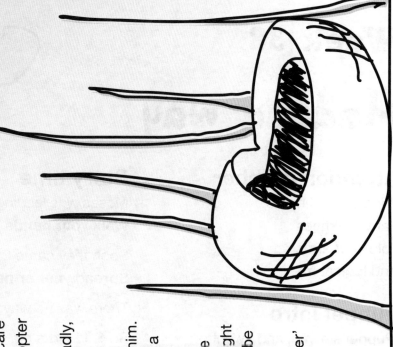

Your child heard this story today …

Miriam had a baby brother called Moses. Some bad people wanted to hurt baby Moses. Miriam's mummy put Moses in a special basket. She hid the basket in the river reeds. Miriam stayed with Moses to watch over him and make sure he was safe. Miriam was a good big sister. She was God's helper!

This story is found in Exodus 2:1–10

Here's a thought …

Here's a (terrible) joke that actually makes a good point … There once was a man stuck on his roof during a flood. While sitting there, a boat came and offered rescue. 'No, that's okay,' he said, 'God will take care of me.' As the water rose higher, a helicopter came along and offered rescue. 'No,' he said again, 'God will take care of me.' Sadly, the water rose and he drowned. Finally, when face-to-face with God, he angrily asked Him why He hadn't taken care of him. God replied, 'Well, I sent you a boat and a helicopter, what else did you want?'

God doesn't sleep. We might even be the pair of hands He sends to help, or we might be the recipient of His care. We need to be ready to receive His help when offered.

'he who watches over you will not slumber' (Psalm 121:3)

Week 38

Made a way

Attention grabber

Wiggle your fingers
Pat your knees
Fold your arms
And look at me!

Puppet intro

[Puppet's name] and I went on an adventure. We walked through grass. We squelched through mud. Then, finally, we came to some water. We didn't have any spare clothes so we couldn't go any further!

Our story today is about how God helped Moses and his friends by moving water to one side.

Story time

Moses was leading some people to a new land. **Walk your hands along your lap.**

Soon they came to a big sea. There was so much water. **Spread your arms wide.**

There was no way around it. **Shake your head.**

So God did a big thing. He pushed the water back **push hands apart** so the people could walk through on dry land. **Walk your hands along your lap.**

God saved the people by moving the water. **Clap and say, 'Hooray!'**

That's the end of the story. Shall we do it again so you can all join in with the actions?

Repeat the story.

This story is found in Exodus 14:21–31

Things to make and do

Play a game called 'Moving Water'.
(**You will need** a bucket full of water, an empty bucket, a collection of plastic toy figures, plastic cups and towels.)

During the group show the children the bucket of water and put the toys in. Say that the toys are getting very wet and they need the children's help! The children need to each use a plastic cup to scoop water out of the bucket and put it into the empty one. When nearly all the water is out, say 'Well done' to the children and ask them to help dry the toys with the towels. If you like, put the toys back into the water and start again! At the end, remind the children of today's story of how God moved the sea and saved Moses.

Made a way

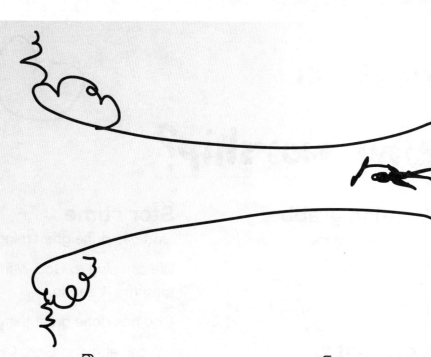

Your child heard this story today …

Moses was leading some people to a new land. Soon they came to a big sea. There was so much water. There was no way around it. So God did a big thing. He pushed the water back so the people could walk through on dry land. God saved the people by moving the water.

This story is found in Exodus 14:21–31

Here's a thought …

When we were small children we could have strange ideas about God. Perhaps we do even now! It's difficult to work out how God can be everywhere at once. It's all too easy to put this Almighty God into a little box – so that we might understand Him. Or we might do so because we think that, somehow, He is not big enough to deal with the problems in our lives.

But the truth is, if He can hold back the sea, He can easily help us deal with the issues and problems we face. In fact, put into perspective next to Him, even the largest ones seem minuscule. His love for you is as big as eternity.

Let Him hold back the sea.

'So do not fear, for I am with you; do not be dismayed, for I am your God. I will strengthen you and help you; I will uphold you with my righteous right hand.' (Isaiah 41:10)

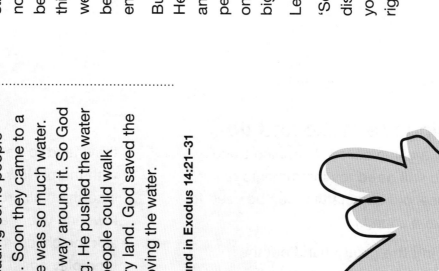

Week 39

Why worship?

Attention grabber

Wiggle your fingers
Pat your knees
Fold your arms
And look at me!

Puppet intro

Do you know what, [puppet's name]? God is *so* good, isn't He?

Puppet nods.

What can we do to say 'Thank You'?

Puppet whispers in your ear.

That's right, we can worship Him!

Today's story is all about how we can worship and praise God.

Story time

God has done great things for me. **Point at yourself.**

We can sing to God. **Mimic holding a microphone, singing, 'La la la.'**

God has done great things for you. **Point at children.**

We can shout to God. **Cup your hands around your mouth and shout, 'Thank You!'**

God has done great things for us. **Sweep your right hand through the air.**

We can clap for God. **Clap enthusiastically.**

God has done great things for everyone. **Sweep your left hand through the air.**

We can dance for God. **Get up and dance.**

That's the end of the story. Shall we do it again so you can all join in with the actions?

Repeat the story.

Things to make and do

Play a game called 'Marching Band'. (**You will need** toy instruments or household objects that can be used to make a sound.)

During the group hand out the instruments and encourage the children to try them out. Tell them that when you raise your hands up they need to be louder and when you lower your hands down they need to be quieter. Have a practice with them! Now tell them to play while you lead them all around the room, raising and lowering your hands. If you like, you could ask the children to swap instruments and then play again. At the end, remind the children that we can thank God for being great by making music and singing to Him.

Why worship?

Your child heard this story today ...

God has done great things for me. We can to sing to God. God has done great things for you. We can shout to God. God has done great things for us. God has done great things for everyone. We can clap for God. We can dance for God.

Here's a thought ...

We all worship something. We might be at a football game, singing our hearts out and raising our hands in the air. We might be at a music event, similarly 'worshipping' a band or artist. We might be at the playground, clapping and praising our child for going down a slide!

So why is worship such an innate part of who we are? Quite simply, God created us this way! We were made to worship Him. Not because He's a big-head, desperate for our affirmation, but because it is *good for us*! (Even secular studies have shown that having a grateful heart is beneficial for us!)

God is good and He does good things in our lives, even when this world tries to dismantle them. He is completely deserving of our praise, even when we're facing hard or painful times, because He is still good nonetheless – He can't *not* be. Let's thank Him for today, for tomorrow and for the day He will finally set things right.

'Sing to GOD a brand-new song. He's made a world of wonders! He rolled up his sleeves, He set things right.' (Psalm 98:1, *The Message*)

Daily devotionals for young children

Ideal for ages 3 to 6, bring the Bible the life with the *Pens* characters, Gloria Glitter-pen, Denzil the Pencil, Charlotte Chalk and a whole host of others! Each with 30 days of Bible readings, stories and simple prayers, help little ones draw closer to God every day with these creative, fun and thought-inspiring devotionals.

God's Peace
ISBN: 978-1-85345-920-7

Praise God!
ISBN: 978-1-85345-921-4

Surprise!
ISBN: 978-1-78259-091-0

God's Way
ISBN: 978-1-78259-263-1

God's Champions
ISBN: 978-1-78259-090-3

Excited!
ISBN: 978-1-78259-264-8

Pens Special Editions

Easter
ISBN: 978-1-85345-652-7

Starting School
ISBN: 978-1-85345-594-0

Pumpkin Party
ISBN: 978-1-85345-990-0

At Christmas
ISBN: 978-1-85345-614-5

Pens Activity Bible
ISBN: 978-1-78259-153-5

Help young readers begin to explore the Bible with these 27 key Bible stories told by the *Pens* characters, each including fun activities such as puzzles, colouring and join the dots games.

Pens Animation Compilation DVD
EAN: 5027957-001541

A compilation of the *Pens* animated stories based on the *Pens Special Editions*. Children will love learning about God through fun stories told by the adorable Pens characters.

For prices and to order, visit www.cwr.org.uk/store